THE LIFE YOU CRAVE

What people are saying about *The Life You Crave*

No matter what difficulties you are going through, this book will embolden you to put your hope in God. It will remind you that you are safe in God's hands and deeply loved by Him. Let this inspiring book inspire you!

James C. Galvin, Ed.D.
Author and Consultant,
Galvin & Associates, Inc.

Once again, Michael Newman demonstrates his prowess at tapping into the vein of our humanity and connecting it to profound truths from God made simple for our understanding. *The Life You Crave* will draw you in because it asks the universal questions of humanity, pulls on the strings in everybody's heart, and invites them to find thirst-quenching relief in the work of God through Jesus.

Mike Sharrow, AfC
Managing Chairman,
C12 Group of Central Texas

In his very clear and relational style, where God's will and grace for every human being always walk side by side, Mike paints for us a picture of who God is and how He gets involved in our daily lives, who and whose we are, and what we're are here on earth for.

Beatriz Hoppe
Multicultural Ministries,
Lutheran Hour Ministries

In a world that craves everything but this, Newman gently persuades the reader to look more deeply at things, to look more intently at things, to see one's life from God's point of view for the life you need, the life we should crave above all else. You won't be disappointed with this book because in it you'll read about an eternal love from God that exists just for you, about a Savior whose gracious love makes an abundant, purposeful, dynamic eternal life possible for all who know and put their trust in Him. (For this, crave on!)

Rev. Gregory Seltz
Speaker,
The Lutheran Hour

Give yourself permission to be surprised by this book when you feel the joy and power in God's love language: "My grace is sufficient" (2 Corinthians 12:9). Yes, it's all about grace.

Eunice Otte
Licensed Professional Counselor

I have known and have respected Rev. Michael Newman for over 15 years, and I am blessed to have him as a friend. His books have helped open my eyes in many ways. If you have missed any of his books, read this one and you will know the blessings of faith that he shares with his readers.

Gloria Jean Kvetko
Gloria Jean's Coffees

I've pulled alongside many a craving in the human heart and laud Mike Newman for once again redirecting our imaginations to the potential God has in mind for us.

Phyllis Wallace
Host,
"Woman to Woman" Syndicated Radio Show

I have had the awesome experience of witnessing Pastor Newman preach, and I've also read his books. He has a tremendous ability to weave our everyday events with happenings in the Bible. Never more has this skill been on display than in this book.

Jim Schwantz
Mayor, Palatine, Illinois;
Former NFL Player

Both in his preaching and in his writing, Pastor Newman has the unique gift of taking biblical truth and applying it to our everyday lives. In this book, he shows how all of humanity, whether biblical heroes or twenty-first-century Americans, have craved one thing—grace. Even more importantly, Pastor Newman points us in the direction to find it.

Bryant Ambelang
President and CEO,
NatureSweet Tomatoes

Trouble and challenges are a reality in our sinful world, but the Lord walks with us through good and bad times. This book reminds us that God has a purpose for our lives and is always in control.

Kay L. Meyer
President and Host,
"Family Shield" Syndicated Radio Program

There is a common conception that deep theology is difficult to understand. Reverend Mike Newman's book *The Life You Crave* proves the fallacy of that idea. His use of creative stories, scriptural insights, and brilliant applications will take you to a deeper and most blessed appreciation of grace. His book is easy to read and deeply inspirational; you will find yourself touched by God's commitment to you.

Rev. Ken Klaus
Speaker Emeritus,
The Lutheran Hour

The task of theological writing is not simply to declare truth, but to convey that truth in a way that is winsome and compelling. With the wisdom of an experienced shepherd, Pastor Newman ably accomplishes this task. Weaving together narratives that spring from the scriptural record and from the headlines, *The Life You Crave* speaks to the basic challenges that confront all people and offers God's timeless truth as the one enduring answer.

Rev. Dr. Joel Bierman
Author and Seminary Professor

THE LIFE YOU CRAVE

It's All about Grace

Michael W. Newman

CONCORDIA PUBLISHING HOUSE · SAINT LOUIS

Published by Concordia Publishing House
3558 S. Jefferson Avenue, St. Louis, MO
63118-3968
1-800-325-3040 • www.cph.org

Text © 2014 Michael W. Newman

www.mnewman.org

Dedication:
To Larry: God gave you the gift of the life you craved.

© iStockphoto.com

Manufactured in the United States of America

Library of Congress Cataloging-in-Publication Data

Newman, Michael W., 1961–

The life you crave : it's all about grace / Michael W. Newman.

p. cm.

Includes index.

1. Christianity and culture. 2. Christian life. 3. Bible.

Daniel—Criticism, interpretation, etc. I. Title.

BR115.C8N478 2014

248.4—dc23

2014028603

1 2 3 4 5 6 7 8 9 10   23 22 21 20 19 18 17 16 15 14

CONTENTS

ONE

> "I have loved
> you with an
> everlasting love."
>
> Jeremiah 31:3

YOUR GREATEST FAN

THE LIFE YOU CRAVE

Do you ever feel like there has to be more to life than what you're living right now? Do you ever wonder if there is something else? After all, it can't be just work, school, bills, and responsibilities. Even the most beautiful vacations, the most enjoyable gatherings with friends, and the most fulfilling relationships seem fleeting and temporary. Is there a bigger reason for being? Can there be a deeper and more meaningful reality? Or is this it?

Please understand, "this" can be pretty nice. This world offers times of absolute delight and euphoria. Falling in love, the birth of a baby, a breathtaking sunset, the majesty of mountains and oceans—"this" can be downright awe-inspiring. But there's another side to "this." It's a shadow side. The frustrations, the valleys of despair, the times of drudgery, and the occasional pointlessness seem to highlight the fact that "this" can't be the whole story. But what is? And how can you connect with a deeper and more meaningful life?

On April 8, 2009, Captain Richard Phillips was taken hostage by a band of Somali pirates. After a botched hijacking of the *Maersk*

Alabama cargo ship off the east coast of Africa, the pirates fled in an enclosed lifeboat. They dragged Captain Phillips inside and set out for the Somali coast. Once there, they planned on demanding millions of dollars for his release.

Phillips endured sweltering temperatures, mock executions, severe beatings, and frightening threats from his captors. His hands were bound so tightly that he still has scars on his wrists. He was a prisoner held by four ruthless, agitated, and greedy men. But in his captivity, Captain Phillips knew there was something more. Even as death seemed near, the captain connected with something no abductor could control. Phillips began to pray for his family. He prayed for strength for his son and daughter. He said his good-byes to his wife. He was comforted by the thoughts of the people he would see in heaven. He focused on a green strut on the bulk-head that was in the shape of a cross. Phillips wondered whether he would make it out of his predicament alive, but he knew the freedom and staying power of something much bigger than his captors.[1]

A young man named Daniel discovered the same thing. You may remember the biblical account of Daniel. He was probably just a teenager when Babylonian invaders broke through the defenses of Jerusalem after a bloody and ruthless siege. Hiding did no good as enemy soldiers flushed the royal family members out of every nook and cranny in the palace complex. Imagine being lined up by foreign enforcers and being subjected to mocking laughter, humili-ating inspection, and an unknown future. As the prisoners were chained together and herded behind the warhorses of Babylon, these children of royalty wondered if they would live or die.

We know of four boys who were taken captive: Daniel, Hananiah, Mishael, and Azariah. Once they made it to Babylon, they were placed under guard and given the bad news: they were no longer royal children of Judah. Their identities were now changed. Their families, traditions, habits, preferences, and wills no longer mattered. Their past was erased. Now they would become Babylonians in service to the king. First, they were stripped of their names. Daniel was renamed Belteshazzar. Hananiah, Mishael, and Azariah were given three names you may recognize: Shadrach, Meshach, and Abednego. The new names paid homage to Babylonian gods. No longer would the God of Israel be part of the boys' lives. Their former lives were over.

As the assimilation process into Babylonian culture began, "Daniel resolved that he would not defile himself with the king's food, or with the wine that he drank. Therefore he asked the chief of the eunuchs to allow him not to defile himself" (Daniel 1:8). Young Daniel didn't want to "sell out" his faith. The practice of eating and drinking only certain foods was a way of honoring God and showing that he didn't buy into the destructive and ungodly practices of Babylonian culture. Daniel wasn't going to throw his faith away. He didn't want to blend in. He believed that bearing witness to the true God was more important than personal comfort. So he asked the man in charge to cut him some slack. Could he and his friends eat vegetables and drink water? If they fared well after ten days, they would be able to continue with their diet and follow the ways of their God. The Bible says, "Now God had caused the official to show favor and compassion to Daniel" (Daniel 1:9 NIV). Daniel was beginning to discover that there was more to life than captivity and anxiety. Even in the worst imprisonment, he discovered remarkable freedom. In dire circumstances, God stepped in with another dimension of reality, a deep connection that would sustain him for decades to come.

The results of Daniel's diet plan were remarkable. Daniel and his friends were not only *as* healthy as the other young men—they were healthier! The king's food couldn't hold a candle to the simple and pure diet of the four young men who resolved to walk faithfully in the footsteps of their Savior God. And this was just the beginning of God's miraculous intervention for His servants stuck in a foreign land.

What is holding you captive? What makes you search for more in life? What causes you to crave something better, something deeper? Do you feel disillusioned or bored? Are you tired of broken relationships? Do you struggle with loneliness or grief? Are you suffering through chronic pain or relentless depression? What about the crazy pace of life, unemployment, personal guilt, broken dreams, or wounds from your past?

The list can go on and on. So many captors try to choke life out of us. To be honest, sometimes we're our own worst enemy. Destructive addictions, hurtful actions, poor decisions, fearful attitudes, and apathetic hearts can drive us into our own sin-broken hostage situation. And we can't free ourselves. With all our strength and savvy, with a world full of technology and know-how, we're still helpless. We're prisoners. But, as Captain Phillips and Daniel experienced, there *is* something more. There is life beyond captivity. There is freedom even in the midst of oppression.

After five days of captivity, Captain Richard Phillips thought his end was near. He knew this situation wouldn't end well. Three

United States navy ships surrounded the sweat- and stench-filled lifeboat. Phillips tried to escape, but he failed and paid the price for it with beatings and abuse. He knew the power of the U.S. military. He knew they wouldn't let the pirates get away with their plan. He wondered if he was going to be destroyed with his captors.

What he didn't know was that a cadre of navy SEALs were perched about a hundred yards in front of the lifeboat, getting ready to rescue the captain. As tempers heated up in the lifeboat and the captors got closer to ending Phillips's life, precision snipers took aim and fired. Suddenly, the blindfolded Phillips heard only silence. Seconds later, a SEAL stormed into the lifeboat and announced the captain's rescue. In shock, traumatized, shaken, and confused, Phillips was ushered aboard a navy destroyer. He was safe. He was rescued. He was now part of the greater reality that had been with him all along. The navy reached in and saved him.

Navy SEALs weren't on hand for Daniel and his friends, but in the agonizing furnace of their enslavement, God reached in with precision help and a clear indication that there was much more to their lives than met the eye. Something bigger was at work. God was connecting with them in a deep and profound way. Even in their captivity, they were part of a greater reality, a reality that transcended the fear and struggle of day-to-day life.

Isn't that the life you crave? Could that life ever be true for you?

GRACE

The answer lies in God's character.

Why does God care about one ship captain hundreds of miles off the coast of Africa? Why did He care about a group of teenagers from the disobedient and corrupt nation of Judah—a nation whose king heard the Word of God, cut it into pieces, and threw it into the fire because he didn't like what it said (Jeremiah 36:23)?

The answer is grace. When I was a kid, the prevailing definition of the word *grace* was "undeserved love." It's a good definition, and the Bible tells us that it is the primary and overriding characteristic of God.

It's true that God is to be feared (Psalm 33:8). He is the Almighty (Genesis 17:1). He is holy (Psalm 99:5). He cannot tolerate sin (Isaiah 61:8). His plan will prevail (Psalm 139:16). He will not share His glory with anyone (Isaiah 42:8). But above all, He loves us with an everlasting love (Jeremiah 31:3).

Even Jesus shared God's principal quality with an inquiring religious leader named Nicodemus. Jesus told him, "For God so loved the world, that He gave His only Son, that whoever believes in Him should not perish but have eternal life. For God did not send His Son into the world to condemn the world, but in order that the world might be saved through Him" (John 3:16–17).

God loved us so much that He couldn't throw us away. Even after the disobedient and selfish rebellion of Adam and Eve in the Garden of Eden, God hung on. Even after unthinkable corruption and godlessness during the time of Noah, God didn't give up. Even after His chosen people turned inward and served themselves instead of their Savior, God stuck with His compassionate plan of salvation. Even after His only Son was tortured, mocked, and killed unjustly on a cross, God raised Jesus to life so that we might have new and everlasting life. Even throughout the ugly swirl of historical unrest, corruption, and violence that has raged after Jesus' resurrection and continues still today, God still loves us. He still seeks us. We can't shake Him loose.

It's grace. Yes, it seems unbelievable—even foolish. But it is the only bright spot in our world. It can bring tears to our eyes, warm our hearts, and make us stand up and cheer. Grace is pure and lavish generosity. God is determined to reach us; He will settle for nothing less than to be connected to us.

In December 2011, Jack Jablonski, a high school sophomore hockey player from Minnesota, was checked hard into the boards and fell to the ice. He lay there motionless while people rushed to his aid. The seventeen-year-old's spinal cord was severed. After a number of surgeries, doctors told Jack that he would never walk again and would never again have full use of his hands and arms. But a prognosis that would have sent others into deep despair motivated Jack to keep fighting. He slowly regained use of his arms, and he received the 2012 CBS Courage in Sports award. Then, in May 2013, just one day before the United States Hockey League's draft, Jack tweeted, "Dear USHL teams, just thought I'd let u know I am eligible for tomorrow's draft. Sincerely Jack Jablonski."

Someone took notice. On the night of the draft, with its last pick, the Chicago Steel tweeted back: "With the final pick the Steel draft Jack Jablonski. Congrats @Jabs_13 on becoming a member of the Steel!"

A paralyzed high school senior was drafted by a professional hockey team! Jablonski shared his surprise and awe: "Best night ever. #steel."[2]

It was undeserved love. It was grace.

The Bible says, "But God shows His love for us in that while we were still sinners, Christ died for us" (Romans 5:8). "But God, being rich in mercy, because of the great love with which He loved us, even when we were dead in our trespasses, made us alive together with Christ—by grace you have been saved" (Ephesians 2:4-5).

We were paralyzed in sin, lifeless in a draining and broken world, hopeless and alone in an existence that always falls short, but God picked us anyway. He pursued us. He stretched His hand into our lives to make a vital and vibrant connection. The Bible says, "But you are a chosen people, a royal priesthood, a holy nation, God's special possession, that you may declare the praises of Him who called you out of darkness into His wonderful light" (1 Peter 2:9 NIV). This is the "more" we need in life. It's the deeper connection and meaning. And it's all because of grace—God's amazing grace.

What We Need Most

In His grace, God digs deeply into our lives to give us what we need the most. Contrary to popular opinion, our greatest need is not wealth, popularity, success, or getting the next tech gadget. It's not even finding a spouse, having a child, or staying healthy. What we really need is to be loved, to matter to someone. But love is not always easy to find.

I'll never forget the day Pam came to visit with me. I had known her for about a year and a half. She was a person who had it all together. She was a polished young professional, steadily climbing the corporate ladder. She was respected by her colleagues for her work ethic and consummate professionalism. She led a balanced life, exercising regularly and participating in running events that raised money for worthy causes. She was articulate. She dressed impeccably. She was friendly and had a smile that brightened a room when she entered it. She attended church faithfully and gave her time to serve in youth ministry. Her life seemed perfect, but through her sobs, I listened to her describe her feelings of inadequacy and failure. Yes, she was successful. But it was success driven by the desire to receive affirmation. For too many years, Pam had tried to fill the hole in her heart with achievement. But after another insult from her father, she fell apart. She could never do enough to please him. She could never succeed enough to receive his affection. But how she yearned for the approving and affirming words of her father! Why wouldn't they come? Why did he continue to bruise her fragile heart? She couldn't stop her tears as she expressed how much she craved the simple gift of her father's unconditional love.

Then there was Bill. Bill had been adopted when he was six years old. Before the adoption, he had bounced from one foster home to another. Then a loving couple took him in and offered their hearts to him. They embraced him fully, thanked God for him every day, and cherished him passionately. But when Bill hit adolescence, he was overcome with curiosity about his birth parents. More than that, he hit a wall of emotion. Why had he been given away? Why had he been rejected? He couldn't shake the thoughts of being cast aside. So he began acting out his frustration, anger, and sadness. Bill's adoptive parents did everything they could to try to help him. Conversation, help to find his birth parents, time with a counselor, gentle love and tough love—they tried it all. But it was no use. Bill began to lash out at his parents. He became loud and violent. Then his bitterness spilled over into self-destructive behavior. He tried to lose himself in drugs and alcohol. He got into trouble with the police. Then he left home. He turned his back on the people who had poured their lives into him. Bill's feelings of rejection ruined his life. He couldn't find the love he craved.

Oh, how we need to be loved! Oh, how we need affirmation! Oh, how we need someone to notice us, to let us know we really matter, and to approve of our lives! We may not admit it all the time, but it is a deep craving.

This craving is what drives our image-driven culture. It causes a feeding frenzy among advertisers and marketers. If clothing or a fragrance or a tech gadget or a car can become something that makes you feel significant, part of the "in" crowd, envied, wanted, cool, or loved—they've got you! They know we don't want to be on the outside, so the images and slogans beckon us to be among the special people who are on the inside.

Unfortunately, the quest to belong, to be included, and to be treasured is a futile chase that never ends. These days, new products become yesterday's news in the blink of an eye. Mobile phone companies have even eliminated two-year contracts because people want to trade in their old phones as soon as the latest one is released. The temporary buzz from getting the newest thing is becoming shorter and shorter in duration. But the craving to feel better about life, to be noticed, and to be significant still rages with ever-growing intensity. People have even killed other people for the latest athletic shoes. And simmering below the violence and aggression is a quiet despair and self-criticism as people feel they can never measure up to the advertised body type or keep up with the latest trend that leads to popularity.

But we keep searching. We keep trying. Broken people, broken families, and a broken culture keep looking for love in all the wrong places.

Our Greatest Fan

This is not what God wants. This is not what God created you to be about. His intention was never to have a self-critical spirit dominate your life. In fact, when you put yourself down, call yourself names, or otherwise demean yourself, God is hurt deeply. He is saddened when you insult His child—you! In God's eyes, you are irreplaceable, carefully crafted by Him, and designed for a unique and noble purpose. You're not an anonymous person in a blob of what we call the general population. You are God's unique individual. God said, "I have called you by name, you are Mine" (Isaiah 43:1). The Bible says, "See what great love the Father has lavished on us, that we should be called children of God! And that is what we are!" (1 John 3:1 NIV).

Of course, there is some truth to our self-loathing. We fail God and others. We don't do what's right. We lean toward selfishness instead of sacrifice. Our imperfections are all too evident. We may be good at hiding our faults and denying our sin, but one honest look in the mirror shows how much we fall short of being truly good, righteous, and pure. We have reason to take a dim view of ourselves. But as you read earlier, while we were still sinners, Christ died for us. Jesus is a friend of sinners. He came to seek and to save the lost. God pursues us. He's our greatest fan.

Young Daniel discovered that. It would sustain him through his life of displaced servitude. God did something very special for these cast-offs in captivity. The closing verses of Daniel 1 tell us:

> As for these four youths, God gave them learning and skill in all literature and wisdom, and Daniel had understanding in all visions and dreams. At the end of the time, when the king had commanded that they

should be brought in, the chief of the eunuchs brought them in before Nebuchadnezzar. And the king spoke with them, and among all of them none was found like Daniel, Hananiah, Mishael, and Azariah. Therefore they stood before the king. And in every matter of wisdom and understanding about which the king inquired of them, he found them ten times better than all the magicians and enchanters that were in all his kingdom. (vv. 17–20)

The kids in shackles now occupied the throne room. The nervous youths were now esteemed by the nation. Even in dire circumstances, God did not abandon them. No, He reached out to them. He connected with them. He brought substance to their lives. He proved that He was their greatest fan.

You may be living in some dire circumstances right now. But can you see God cheering you on? Can you sense His encouragement? Even as you muddle through a place you'd rather not be, are you hearing God's cries of promise and support? Are you receiving His big and small gestures of reassurance? Do you realize that God is the founding member of your fan club? that He wears your team colors, waves the foam fan hand on your behalf, and is a season ticket holder to all your games?

Sometimes, it's hard to believe, but this is the life God gives. And it started at the very beginning. In Genesis 1 we're told:

Then God said, "Let Us make man in Our image, after Our likeness. And let them have dominion over the fish of the sea and over the birds of the heavens and over the livestock and over all the earth and over every creeping thing that creeps on the earth." So God created man in His own image, in the image of God He created him; male and female He created them. (vv. 26–27)

God made us in His image. Did you ever wonder what that means? Over the centuries, theologians and thinkers have given a number of answers. Some have said that being made in God's image and likeness means that we, as humans, have a rational soul. We can think, reason, and discern. We have a conscience. We can create, invent, and innovate. We can express emotion and care. The "image of God" has been considered by others as an indication that human beings have a unique knowledge of God. They share in God's holy will, His thinking, and His attitudes.

Much of that is probably true, but there may be more packed into being made in God's image. In Genesis 5, we hear a similar expression: "When Adam had lived 130 years, he fathered a son in his own likeness, after his image, and named him Seth" (v. 3). This expression is a family expression. It connotes a genetic bond, a DNA link. Being made in the image and likeness of someone means you're not a stranger. No, you're close. You're family.

Genesis 9 gives us even more information: "Whoever sheds the blood of man, by man shall his blood be shed, for God made man in His own image" (v. 6). This verse tells us that being made in the image of God means that our lives are precious. They're important. They can't be treated lightly or tossed aside as an expendable commodity.

Part of the meaning of being made "in the image of God" is that we're loved by God. Above all creation, human beings are treasured. God established a special love relationship with us. That is underscored when we see that the word for "image" in the Bible (*tselem* in Hebrew) is also used for the "images" or idols people devoted their lives to. People adored these false gods. They gave them special places in their homes. They offered sacrifices to them. To paraphrase Martin Luther's explanation of the First Commandment, they feared, loved, and trusted in their "images" above all things.

God made us in His "image." He loves us above all things—above all creation. In a sense, He "worships the ground we walk on." He's our greatest fan. That's why, after Adam and Eve fouled up the plan by rebelling against God in the Garden of Eden, God rebooted the flow of history and promised His own Son as a substitute to pay the price for the system crash we caused. He promised the suffering and death of Jesus when He said, "I will put enmity between you and the woman, and between your offspring and her offspring; He shall bruise your head, and you shall bruise His heel" (Genesis 3:15).

Even Jesus is called "the image of God." Colossians 1:15 says, "He is the image of the invisible God, the firstborn of all creation." Jesus is God's beloved Son. This "image of God" talk has some precious love packed into it. It underscores that from the beginning, God was our greatest fan.

I will confess to you that I am a Chicago Cubs fan. I grew up in the Chicago area and began attending Cubs games when I was a boy. During those days, fans could get into Wrigley Field early to watch the players go through batting practice. As players milled around on the field, we could hang over the infield wall and beg for autographs. We brought hats, gloves, and baseballs for the players to sign. It was a dream come true when a uniformed baseball "icon" approached us and graced us with an autograph. After giving profuse thanks to the player, we autograph seekers looked at the signature and tried to figure out who in the world had just signed our precious memento. We loved and adored those Cubbies! By the way, the Greek word for "image" in the New Testament is *icon.* The word is packed with adoration.

My life as a Cub fan, however, is no match for that of Ronnie "Woo Woo" Wickers. Ronnie was born in 1941 and has attended almost every Chicago Cubs home game since the late 1950s. He earned his nickname from the "woo" sound he makes when he cheers loudly for his precious team. During some lean years in employment, Ronnie even managed to get tickets to games while he was homeless. He preferred to miss a meal or to sleep outside rather than miss a Cubs home game. No sacrifice was too great for Ronnie's fandom to continue.[3]

God is the same way about you. He is a "superfan," preferring to sacrifice everything rather than miss out on loving you. Of course, God never suffered lean years of employment. God never became homeless, as Ronnie did. But we did. In the Garden of Eden, we fouled up. We human beings decided that we would rather *be* God than *follow* God. We rejected our Creator and struck out on our own. And the result of that rebellious decision resembled the record of the Chicago Cubs: a losing one. Something very serious happened in our relationship with God when Adam and Eve chose to eat from the tree of the knowledge of good and evil. Dire spiritual consequences resulted. Our lives were in grave danger. What was God's reaction? Leave it to our "Superfan" to do this for us:

❋   To promise a deliverer

❋ To keep the promise going by putting a family on an ark while the world drowned in sin

❋ To overpower an Egyptian despot and bring people out of slavery with miraculous works so the world could see God's rescuing heart

❋ To abide with His precious people in the wilderness, appearing to them and providing for them every step of the way

❋ To stick with them even when they fouled up and rejected Him

❋ To plead with them when they were unfaithful

❋ To send His only Son to live a perfect life for us and to carry the blame and punishment for our sins

❋ To allow His Son to be put to death on a cross so that we would never have to suffer what our sins deserved

❋ To raise His Son to life so that we could share in the gift of eternal life

❋ To speak to us through His Word and deliver all His gifts through the tools of Baptism and the Lord's Supper

❋ To entrust us with a message of hope that every life craves

Leave it to our Superfan to go to such great lengths for the object of His affection. But God's love for us isn't blind. It's not an absentminded passion that sees the world or our lives through rose-colored glasses. No, God sees the truth and is honest with us about the truth—just like Ronnie "Woo Woo" Wickers. You see, Wickers starts his day by paying a visit to one of his favorite places: a statue of Jesus on the campus of Loyola University. He stops by to pray for the world, to pray for himself, and to pray for the Cubs. Ronnie said, "There were a few times when I had no other place to go and I slept behind that statue. It's a special place to me. No matter the weather, I go there and ask God for peace. And a World Series."[4]

I'll be the first one to acknowledge that the lovable-loser Chicago Cubs need divine intervention. So do we—each one of us. And God is up front and honest with us about this truth in a refreshing way. The rhythm of His Word to us is a steady cadence of sin and grace, honesty about our shortcomings and honesty about His rescue, the painful truth of our helplessness, and the refreshing revelation of our salvation. God pulls no punches in putting the full weight of His Law upon us—and letting us know we deserve it. He then spares no effort to bring the fullness of His grace to our lives, the Gospel of surprising new life through Jesus, which we neither earned nor deserved. Ephesians 2 tells us, "And you were dead in the trespasses and sins. . . . But God, being rich in mercy, because of the great love with which He loved us, even when we were dead in our trespasses, made us alive together with Christ— by grace you have been saved" (Ephesians 2:1, 4–5).

Living in Reality

God cares enough to tell the truth. Advertisers will exaggerate claims. Self-help books will inflate your abilities. Friends may gloss over your imperfections. Philosophies and ideologies will bask in egotistical brilliance. World religions will chart out personal pathways to perfect peace and divine realization. But only the true God will get in your face and tell you that you're an imperfect, helpless, and fallen corpse in dire need of rescue and resuscitation. That's part of the Bible's message. And it's the truth. Without a Savior, we are cellar-dwelling, last-place losers with no hope of victory in life. One look in the mirror confirms this assessment. Do you see your imperfection? Will you own up to your failures? Can you acknowledge that you can't cut it on your own? And as soon as we admit that we're not championship material, God steps in with the news of Jesus. That's another part of the Bible's truthful and important message.

In Acts 4, Peter and John were being grilled by church officials about how they healed a crippled beggar at the temple gates. Crowds of people who understood the reality of their need in life believed in the apostles' message of Jesus' resurrection for them. But the church leaders didn't budge. Finally, in response to their questions, Peter spoke to them about Jesus. He said, "There is salvation in no one else, for there is no other name under heaven given among men by which we must be saved" (v. 12).

Did you hear what Peter said? There is salvation in no one else because no one has ever provided a Savior. There are plenty of positive thinkers. There are bunches of people who won't level with you. There is a deep well of self-deception and denial in each of us. There are religions, philosophies, and ideologies by the bucketful. There are salespeople and advertisers who will tell you what you want to hear. But there is only one Savior. His name is Jesus. He's your greatest fan. He reaches out to you to give you a life that has more depth, fullness, substance, and meaning than you could ever imagine. He connects with you in creative and dynamic ways.

Are you ready to hear more? Are you ready to discover God's

remarkable grace for your life? Are you ready to receive the blessing of the life you crave?

Notes

1. Richard Phillips, *A Captain's Duty* (New York: Hyperion, 2010), 222–23.

2. www.foxsportsnorth.com/nhl/minnesota-wild/story/-USHL-team-honors-Jack-Jablonski-with-fi?blockID=900097

3. sports.espn.go.com/espn/eticket/story?num=3578251&page=cubs100

4. Ibid.

STUDY GUIDE FOR CHAPTER ONE

YOUR GREATEST FAN

1. What tends to hold you "captive," keeping you away from God and the life He gives?

2. Read 1 Corinthians 15:17–22. How has God freed you, both from the deadly captors of sin and death and from the circumstances in life that try to "hold you hostage"?

3. This chapter offered a definition of God's grace as "undeserved love." What definitions of grace are you familiar with, and why are they meaningful to you?

4. Read Ephesians 2:8–10. What do these verses say about God's grace in our lives?

5. To what lengths do people go in order to feel significant and loved? Talk about the temptations of our culture and the temptations you experience in your daily life.

6. God is completely honest with us in His Word. Read Romans 3:10–20 and discuss what this honest message says about us and about what we deserve from God.

7. Read Romans 3:21–24. This is another part of God's honest message to us. What does it mean for our lives?

8. God's Law makes our sin and shortcomings very evident in our lives. The blessing of the Gospel reveals the Good News of our salvation in Jesus. Take another look at Acts 4:12. What is unique about Jesus compared with the religions, ideologies, and philosophies of the world?

9. Read Romans 5:6–8. Discuss how these verses show God's tenacious and gracious reach into our lives.

TWO

> "For I know the plans I have for you," declares the LORD, "plans to prosper you and not to harm you, plans to give you hope and a future."
>
> Jeremiah 29:11–12 (NIV)

YOUR AMAZING PURPOSE

HENRY'S LIFE

It wasn't a good day for Henry Dunant when he received the news that he had to leave college because his grades weren't good enough. Henry, age 21, was the firstborn son in his family. His parents were influential and successful residents of Geneva, Switzerland. What would they say? How would the community react? What would he do with his life?

Henry's parents were kind and loving. They raised him in a devout Christian home. They were wonderful examples of putting Jesus' love into action. Henry's father, a businessman, was also a dedicated servant of people who were forgotten and disenfranchised. He volunteered significant amounts of time to help children at an orphanage and to minister to men in a local prison. Henry's mother invested her time reaching out to the poor and ill. They instilled this self-sacrificial spirit in their firstborn son.

By the time Henry was eighteen years old, he had joined the Geneva Society for Almsgiving. When he was nineteen, he gathered a group of friends who met regularly to study the Bible and to serve the less fortunate. Henry followed in his parents' footsteps by visiting the imprisoned and helping the poor. His heart pulled him in the direction of serving others with the love of Christ, but he knew his focus wouldn't pay the bills. How would he make a living?

After his unexpected departure from college, Henry started an internship at a bank. He did well enough to earn a position there. His job sent him on interesting business journeys to Italy and North Africa. But while he worked, he continued to reach out to the community. When he was twenty-four, Henry established the Geneva chapter of the YMCA. Three years later, in 1855, he participated in the founding of the international organization. Henry was making a big impact.

But he didn't feel that way. In 1856, Henry dug more deeply into his business ventures. Having experienced some success, he took the risk of starting a venture in North Africa, using a land grant for his home base. Unable to procure water rights in the French colony, Henry decided to cut through the frustrating red tape by appealing to the French emperor, Napoleon III. Henry traveled to Italy to meet with him personally.

That's when another detour appeared in Henry Dunant's life. Arriving in the Northern Italy town of Solferino in June 1859, Dunant stumbled into the aftermath of a battle between the French and Austrians. Twenty-three thousand soldiers lay wounded, dying, or dead on the battlefield. But no one was providing any help. Henry's heart to serve was moved to immediate action. He rallied local citizens to come to the aid of the wounded. He sent away for medical supplies so proper help could be given. He oversaw the construction of temporary hospitals to house the battered and shocked soldiers. He convinced the French to release Austrian prisoners of war who were doctors. He even persuaded the area's residents to help whoever was in need—even soldiers, who were considered enemies. Henry threw himself into serving others while his attention to business waned.

When Dunant arrived back in Geneva, he wrote *A Memory of Solferino*, an account of his experience there. Publishing the book at his own expense, Henry traveled throughout Europe to promote the book's main ideas. He believed that each country should establish a neutral organization of volunteers that cared for victims of battle and natural disasters. By 1863, Henry Dunant, with a committee of four others, founded the organization called The Red Cross. By 1864, Henry's movement to care for wounded soldiers resulted in the signing of the First Geneva Convention. Henry was making a big impact.

But he still didn't feel that way. Because he devoted so much time and money to his humanitarian efforts, his business failed. Investors were left unpaid and unhappy. Henry went bankrupt. He was no longer welcome in Geneva. He was ousted from the International Red Cross Committee. He was removed from the YMCA. Then his mother died. Henry left Geneva in poverty, shame, and sadness. At only thirty-nine years of age, Henry began to live the life of a beggar in obscurity. This season of suffering would last for nearly thirty years.

There are times when it is difficult to understand life's struggles and setbacks. There are times when we wonder what God is doing. It is during those times that we are called to trust in Him. C. H. Spurgeon, a renowned English preacher who lived during Henry Dunant's era, is credited with saying, "God is too good to be unkind and He is too wise to be confused, and if I cannot trace His hand I can always trust His heart." King Solomon declared, "Trust in the LORD with all your heart, and do not lean on your own understanding. In all your ways acknowledge Him, and He will make straight your paths" (Proverbs 3:5–6). But trusting God is not always an easy journey.

PURPOSE AND STRUGGLE

The prophet Daniel must have felt similar to Henry Dunant. Daniel was an up-and-coming member of the royal family in Jerusalem. But his life quickly came crashing down. As a teenager in captivity in Babylon, life was filled with opposition, pressure, and trouble. There were no shared values in his new surroundings. The goal of every Babylonian who entered his life was to change him from a follower of the God of Abraham, Isaac, and Jacob to a follower of the gods of this hostile and strange nation. Life was not easy. Daniel would ride this roller coaster of sadness, uncertainty, and pain until the day he died as an old man.

Shortly after Daniel's arrival and indoctrination into Babylonian culture, King Nebuchadnezzar had a troubling dream. He summoned his magicians, enchanters, and dream interpreters. Nebuchadnezzar must have become suspicious of his spiritual advisers. Perhaps Daniel and his friends planted a seed of doubt in the king's mind. Perhaps the Holy Spirit was working on Nebuchadnezzar after he witnessed something very special in the young captives from Jerusalem. So the king approached his advisers with caution. This is what happened:

> [King Nebuchadnezzar] said to them, "I have had a dream that troubles me and I want to know what it means." Then the astrologers answered the king, "May

the king live forever! Tell your servants the dream, and we will interpret it." The king replied to the astrologers, "This is what I have firmly decided: If you do not tell me what my dream was and interpret it, I will have you cut into pieces and your houses turned into piles of rubble. But if you tell me the dream and explain it, you will receive from me gifts and rewards and great honor. So tell me the dream and interpret it for me." (Daniel 2:3–6 NIV)

Nebuchadnezzar was not the compromising type. The king's spiritual advisers insisted that the king first tell them the dream, but Nebuchadnezzar refused. Nebuchadnezzar was knee-deep in testing the ability of his so-called spiritual team. Exasperated, the advisers said:

There is no one on earth who can do what the king asks! No king, however great and mighty, has ever asked such a thing of any magician or enchanter or astrologer. What the king asks is too difficult. No one can reveal it to the king except the gods, and they do not live among humans. (Daniel 2:10–11 NIV)

Can you hear God snickering in the heavens? The God who is with us, who comes down to help us, who faithfully dwells with people for salvation, who appeared to Moses in the burning bush, who manifested Himself as a pillar of cloud and a pillar of fire for the people of Israel, who met with Moses on the mountain, and whose presence filled the tabernacle and the temple was getting ready to make a big point. But for Daniel, the story hadn't ended. First, Nebuchadnezzar lost his temper and made the situation very grim. Daniel 2 tells us:

> Because of this the king was angry and very furious,
> and commanded that all the wise men of Babylon be
> destroyed. So the decree went out, and the wise men
> were about to be killed; and they sought Daniel and
> his companions, to kill them. (vv. 12–13)

Daniel was experiencing a Henry Dunant moment. Life was crashing in. Nothing looked promising. All seemed lost. When the king's guard appeared at Daniel's door with a sword, Daniel reasoned with him. The Bible says he spoke to the guard with "prudence and discretion" (v. 14), with "wisdom and tact" (v. 14 NIV). After hearing the details about the dream debacle, Daniel went directly to the king to ask for time. Then Daniel hightailed it home. He explained the situation to his three friends and asked them to join him in prayer, pleading for mercy from the God of heaven—the true God—regarding the mystery of this dream.

It's interesting to note that throughout the Book of Daniel, Daniel is called by his Hebrew name most of the time. In chapter 2, Hananiah, Mishael, and Azariah are also called by their Hebrew names. It is as if God was affirming their true identity. They may have been captives. They may have been immersed in Babylonian culture and surroundings. But they were still children of the God of heaven. Their names still gave witness to their Savior. Even in their terrible struggle, they still had purpose.

So Daniel and his friends prayed and pleaded with God into the night.

Henry Dunant did not respond to adversity in that way. Henry became sad and somewhat bitter. He struggled with depression and developed paranoia about his creditors. He railed against his religious upbringing and was thought to have become an agnostic.

Then, in 1895, at age 67, Henry suddenly experienced a reversal of fortune. An article was written in which it was recognized that he had been instrumental in founding the Red Cross. Suddenly, he received worldwide acclaim. He was awarded several prizes and honors, including the first Nobel Peace Prize. He received an honorary doctorate from the University of Heidelberg. Prize money filled his bank account. He was befriended by advocates who protected the funds from creditors and naysayers. But Henry never spent any of the money. He stayed in a small nursing home in the Swiss village of Heiden. According to his wishes, he had no funeral when he died. He asked that he be carried to his grave "like a dog."[1]

Life is not easy. The sinful and broken world in which we live doles out heartache and pain by the bucketful. And we cause plenty of sorrow too. Years ago, author Erma Bombeck wrote a book called *If Life Is a Bowl of Cherries, What Am I Doing in the Pits?* The title captures the reality of life on this side of heaven. God gives us great care while we journey on this earth. He provides beauty and blessing. He gives us tastes of heaven in His Word and Sacraments. But heaven is not on earth. No matter how much we want everything we do to go "up and to the right," that's not the way life develops. No, there are ups and downs. There is progress, and there are setbacks. Sometimes, the worst of life happens when we think the best of life should be taking place. Sometimes, trials cripple us when we're expecting times of peace and relaxation.

People are the same way. Throughout my ministry, I've realized that God's people do not follow a uniform track of development. The Church cannot expect to mass-produce gung-ho leaders for every new ministry initiative. While some followers of Christ step into ministry responsibilities with vigor, there are a good number of God's people who are "smoldering wicks" and "bruised reeds" (see Isaiah 42:3; Matthew 12:20)—fragile people whose lives slip and slide through times of debilitating adversity, comebacks of success, and the middle ground of trying to keep it all together. The Bible tells us that Jesus came to make sure these bruised reeds are not broken and these smoldering wicks are not snuffed out. This is the reality we face. Jesus said clearly, "In this world you will have trouble. But take heart! I have overcome the world" (John 16:33 NIV). Trouble is a reality in this world. Jesus has overcome it through His life, death, and resurrection for us, but as long as we're in this world, we will experience trial and tribulation. That's why the Bible encourages us in our journeys of faith:

> Therefore, my beloved brothers, be steadfast, immovable, always abounding in the work of the Lord, knowing that in the Lord your labor is not in vain. (1 Corinthians 15:58)

> Let us not become weary in doing good, for at the proper time we will reap a harvest if we do not give up. (Galatians 6:9 NIV)

I think Daniel understood this. When everything started to collapse, Daniel did his best to represent the character of God as he dealt with the guard and the king: he reached out to his fellow believers and fled to God's mercy in prayer. The God of heaven was his refuge and strength in times of trouble (Psalm 46:1). Trouble was part of his reality. Struggle paid regular visits. But he knew God had a purpose and plan for him.

In Daniel 9:2, Daniel referenced Jeremiah's prophecy that God's people would be in captivity for seventy years. Daniel paid close attention to the Scriptures. He trusted God's Word. He placed his hope in God's promises. Jeremiah 29:10 says, "For thus says the LORD: When seventy years are completed for Babylon, I will visit you, and I will fulfill to you My promise and bring you back to this place."

I believe Daniel read the verse that follows and trusted it too: "'For I know the plans I have for you,' declares the LORD, 'plans to prosper you and not to harm you, plans to give you hope and a future'" (Jeremiah 29:11 NIV). The Hebrew word for "plans" used here can mean "thoughts, intentions, a design." Daniel knew that God was thinking about him. Even when the situation was desperate and nothing looked very promising, God had him in mind and thought about his purpose.

The same is true for you. Psalm 8:4 declares, "What is man that You are mindful of him, and the son of man that You care for him?" God remembers you. He thinks about you. He has plans for you—not just the big, life-changing, high-ambition plans you may construct and hope for, but the little things for each ordinary day. Even when life feels lousy, God hasn't forgotten about you. God still has an important purpose for you. It may seem small to you, but you're irreplaceable to God. Even if your life consists only of having a heart that beats and lungs that breathe, you are still an important part of God's precious plan. He thinks about you and treasures you. He's glad you're here.

This may not have been the mind-set of Henry Dunant. Henry may have bought in to a theological mind-set that believed the fullness of God's kingdom could come to fruition on earth, that believers in Christ were able to have constantly improving sanctified lives that reached ever-greater levels of holiness. Dunant may have overlooked the fact that struggle and pain still plague God's people, that the devil causes havoc because he knows his time is short, that our sinful flesh still weighs heavily upon us, and that hard times rage but do not necessarily point to God's absence.

Remember the account of Jesus and the disciples encountering a man born blind, which is recorded in the Gospel of John. The disciples assumed that the man's malady had been caused by a family sin. John tells it this way:

> As [Jesus] passed by, He saw a man blind from birth. And His disciples asked Him, "Rabbi, who sinned, this man or his parents, that he was born blind?" Jesus answered, "It was not that this man sinned, or his parents, but that the works of God might be displayed in him." (9:1–3)

Jesus cut through the narrow and naïve spiritual mind-set of His followers. The messiness of sin and chaos does not mean God is absent. No, God digs into the mess and is even glorified through it! Jesus was born in a barn. He was laid in a feeding trough. He walked the treacherous pathways of this earth. He was a friend of sinners. He suffered what we suffer. The Book of Hebrews declares, "Therefore [Jesus] had to be made like His brothers in every respect, so that He might become a merciful and faithful high priest in the service of God, to make propitiation for the sins of the people. For because He Himself has suffered when tempted, He is able to help those who are being tempted" (2:17–18). Your life's mess does not mean God has abandoned you. Your suffering and pain do not eliminate God's purpose from your life. Henry Dunant may have grown bitter because of that tension, but the prophet Daniel grew closer to God and saw God receive glory and honor during the worst of times.

Your Amazing Purpose

Daniel and his friends spent the day in prayer, pleading, begging, and imploring God to be merciful in this very unusual and nerve-racking predicament. Whoever heard of a king demanding that his wise men tell him what he dreamed and interpret the dream? This was not in the Babylonian Orientation Guide. No one covered this in the Captivity Survival Manual. This was new territory for the boys from Jerusalem. And if Nebuchadnezzar's insiders were stumped, how could outsiders like Daniel, Hananiah, Mishael, and Azariah figure out this one? So they prayed into the night. They went to their refuge and strength, their present help in times of trouble. Their faith was growing up fast.

What did God do? How did He respond? Contrary to the opinion of the king's magicians and enchanters, God decided to come down to the mess. Half of one little verse covers this remarkable response of God, this miraculous intervention by the King of kings, who decided to draw close to His people: "Then the mystery was revealed to Daniel in a vision of the night" (Daniel 2:19).

This response was not just a fluke. It wasn't simply a bailout maneuver by God as He responded to a crisis situation. This was God's plan. It was His plan for Daniel, for Daniel's fellow prisoners, and for the kingdom of Babylon. God wanted His people to be a light for the nations. He wanted to win the hearts of the world. The people of Israel hadn't done very well in this calling. They became self-centered, corrupt, and unjust. They cheated the poor and helpless. They neglected the widows, orphans, and disenfranchised. They worshiped other gods and compromised their faith. Eventually, God removed His hand of protection and sent His people into captivity.

But God's gracious mission for the world endured. So, through a frightened bunch of teenagers, God accomplished His plan of salvation. The reason for Daniel's existence was to display to the world the truth of the God of heaven. Daniel was a pressured and frightened prisoner for the express purpose of letting all people see the steadfast love of the true God. Daniel and his friends would be used by God to change the hearts of the people they encountered. Their purpose was to make an eternal difference for people all over the world.

That's your purpose too. You're not here by accident. Your life is not the result of an assembly-line production of people. You're not a widget with a number, occupying space anonymously until you fade into nothingness. God created you for His glory so that heads will turn to Him and acknowledge Him as Lord of all. In the Book of Isaiah, God spoke about the rescue of His people from the very captivity Daniel was enduring in Babylon. As God called His people out of bondage, He also expressed their purpose:

> "Bring My sons from afar and My daughters from the end of the earth, everyone who is called by My name, whom I created for My glory, whom I formed and made." (Isaiah 43:6–7)

The apostle Paul reinforced this grand purpose when he said, "So, whether you eat or drink, or whatever you do, do all to the glory of God" (1 Corinthians 10:31).

If you know and believe in your Greatest Fan, the one and only Savior God, your purpose here on earth is to give God glory, to point people to Him so that they can know Him too. Everything we do is meant to display the marvelous and amazing character of the Lord of all and to open eyes to the new life He graciously gives.

Yes, I said *everything* we do. Martin Luther taught that God is operating in our everyday activities. He said that His redeemed people can be "masks" for God—God working through human beings to effect His will. Our actions are vehicles of God's love to others. In fact, Luther loved to think that the most common actions of people could very well contain some of the best secrets God has to offer, noble "jewels" that others consider ordinary and unimportant.[2] God utilizes our ordinary lives to share His love, to show Himself through us. He gets tangled up in your life and uses you as an instrument of His work.

Sometimes, that work is very challenging. Infiltrating nooks and crannies of difficulty, reaching into dark corners of pain, and serving the lonely and forgotten is not easy. Admission to those places is granted only by paying a high price. There is only one way to gain entry to a dialysis lab. Being God's shining light in a nursing home comes with great sacrifice and struggle. Relating with total understanding to a person whose child ended his life happens only after traveling a dark and foreboding valley of death and grief.

You may think God has forgotten you. But He may be embracing you as a missionary to the most difficult places imaginable. Your calling—even the most difficult—may be a mask of God's far-reaching love for people who would otherwise feel totally lost or be completely forgotten. No matter what circumstances fill your life, God's amazing, important, significant, and eternal purpose for you still endures.

I wonder if this is what the apostles Paul and Peter meant when they referenced our sharing in the sufferings of Christ. Paul said, "For as we share abundantly in Christ's sufferings, so through Christ we share abundantly in comfort too" (2 Corinthians 1:5).

Peter noted, "But rejoice insofar as you share Christ's sufferings, that you may also rejoice and be glad when His glory is revealed" (1 Peter 4:13).

Jesus suffered more than we can ever imagine. Physically, emotionally, and spiritually, Jesus plunged into the depths of extreme agony. But He still knew He was fulfilling His calling, the purpose given to Him by God the Father. Difficulty did not eliminate purpose. Even as He faced the worst and despaired of life itself, Jesus knew He was still in the middle of God's purpose and plan. He prayed in the Garden of Gethsemane: "Father, if You are willing, remove this cup from Me. Nevertheless, not My will, but Yours, be done" (Luke 22:42).

Jesus understood that suffering did not negate purpose. He knew this from early on. In Luke 2, we hear that Jesus was growing up. After Jesus was presented in the temple as an infant, we are told:

> And when they had performed everything according to the Law of the Lord, they returned into Galilee, to their own town of Nazareth. And the child grew and became strong, filled with wisdom. And the favor of God was upon Him. (vv. 39–40)

The Greek word used here for "grew" is a word that means "to increase" and "to be fruitful." The Greek word is *auxano*. It is a positive-growth word, indicating forward and upward movement. The same word is used to describe Joshua, the successor to Moses. God "exalted" Joshua:

> On that day the LORD exalted Joshua in the sight of all Israel, and they stood in awe of him just as they had

stood in awe of Moses, all the days of his life. (Joshua
4:14)

This was the kind of growth you'd expect from a young man—
especially the Son of God, the Messiah. But this is not the only
word used in the Bible to describe Jesus' growth. Luke tells us the
whole story. Jesus' years of growing up were not just peaches and
cream. After He dilly-dallied in Jerusalem, spending extra time in
the temple listening to the teachers and asking them questions, Jesus' worried parents found Him and brought Him home. Back at
home, Jesus submitted to His parents. Luke 2:52 (NIV) says, "And
Jesus grew in wisdom and stature, and in favor with God and man."
The word for "grew" used in verse 52 is different from the word
used in verse 40. It is the Greek word *prokopto*. The word is related
to a nautical term that means "to make headway in spite of blows."[3]
The term communicates progress, but it also characterizes that
progress as not coming very easily. Suffering and struggle filled Jesus' days—even from His youth. But through it all, Jesus knew His
Father had an important purpose for His life. He knew His Father
was thinking about Him and had a plan in mind.

The same is true for you. You may feel like you're plowing
through high seas, buffeted by wind and waves at every moment.
You may be weary, and you may wonder why God doesn't make it
a little bit easier for you. Daniel wondered the same thing. But after
the dream episode with Nebuchadnezzar, Daniel may have started
to catch on to God's glorious purpose of sharing His majesty with
the world.

After God revealed the mystery to Daniel, Daniel praised God
for His grace and blessing. Daniel realized that God was truly God
and that He was in control of all things—even hotheaded kings.

Daniel understood that God was good and gracious, showing him mercy and responding to his prayers. So Daniel hurried to the king's guard and asked to be taken to the king. In the king's presence, Daniel lived out his purpose. He introduced the king of Babylon to the true God:

> Daniel answered the king and said, "No wise men, enchanters, magicians, or astrologers can show to the king the mystery that the king has asked, but there is a God in heaven who reveals mysteries, and He has made known to King Nebuchadnezzar what will be in the latter days." (Daniel 2:27–28)

"There is a God in heaven who reveals mysteries." Don't you love it? A pagan king who would never qualify for an evangelism prospect list and who never would be accessible to the visitation committee at church was hearing the Word of life!

Daniel then explained the dream about a tall statue made of a variety of materials, from gold to clay. He told Nebuchadnezzar about the coming kingdoms and the eternal kingdom of God. He let Nebuchadnezzar know that the God of heaven was the one who gave him power, but while earthly kingdoms fall, the eternal kingdom that God establishes will vanquish all other kingdoms and will never fall.

What was Nebuchadnezzar's reaction? He was probably blown away that Daniel could tell him what he had dreamed! With jaw squarely on the floor, the king fell down before Daniel and said, "Truly, your God is God of gods and Lord of kings, and a revealer of mysteries, for you have been able to reveal this mystery" (Daniel 2:47). A seed was planted. Soon, Nebuchadnezzar would be proclaiming the true God to his entire kingdom.

Daniel was in the middle of God's amazing purpose. He had been sent by God into some very risky territory. God does that. He takes risks with our lives. He puts us out there just like He put His own Son out there. He takes the greatest risks for the salvation of the people He loves. His own Son was put to death and buried. Jesus' battered body was sealed in a tomb. It looked like all was lost. But then came the resurrection.

The apostle Paul said that each of us, in Baptism, was taken through this risky journey to new life:

> Do you not know that all of us who have been baptized into Christ Jesus were baptized into His death? We were buried therefore with Him by baptism into death, in order that, just as Christ was raised from the dead by the glory of the Father, we too might walk in newness of life. For if we have been united with Him in a death like His, we shall certainly be united with Him in a resurrection like His. (Romans 6:3–6)

This is the life you crave, isn't it? It's unpredictable, miraculous, unlike anything the world can produce, filled with significance and purpose beyond our imagination, bringing an eternal impact to each life around us. This is a life that goes beyond the ordinary. It is a supernatural adventure that makes a real difference. It is a journey that brings surprises—results we could never anticipate. Daniel found himself in the throne room of the king. He never wanted to be there, but there he was, speaking to a king about the King of kings. Only God could craft such a plan.

What is happening in your life that you never expected? How might God use it to share His love and care with someone new? How might God use the joy and the sorrow, the delight and the struggle to introduce someone to Him? By God's grace, there is much more than just the mess. You have an amazing purpose.

SENT TO SERVE

This was God's method of operation from the very beginning. When God created Adam and Eve, He also told them, "Be fruitful and multiply and fill the earth and subdue it" (Genesis 1:28). This was not just a command to have a bunch of kids. God gave the first humans a high calling to let their children know about Him. Malachi 2:15 reinforces this mission purpose. Referring to husbands and wives, the prophet said, "Did [God] not make them one, with a portion of the Spirit in their union? And what was the one God seeking? Godly offspring. So guard yourselves in your spirit, and let none of you be faithless to the wife of your youth." God wanted husbands and wives to be vehicles of His love. He delegated the holy calling of sharing the Good News to parents so they could produce godly offspring.

God even continued this mission purpose when the chips were down. After Adam and Eve disobeyed God and aligned themselves with the devil by eating from the tree of the knowledge of good and evil, God stepped in. He promised a Savior (Genesis 3:15). He outlined consequences of suffering and struggle for both the snake and the first humans. Then He did something that displayed His heart and character. Genesis 3 tells it this way:

> And the LORD God made for Adam and for his wife garments of skins and clothed them. Then the LORD God said, "Behold, the man has become like one of Us in knowing good and evil. Now, lest he reach out his

hand and take also of the tree of life and eat, and live forever—" therefore the LORD God sent him out from the garden of Eden to work the ground from which he was taken. (vv. 21–23)

First, God sacrificed animals to clothe Adam and Eve. This shedding of blood served as a substitute for their own deaths as a consequence of sin. These sacrifices would continue until Jesus became the substitutionary sacrifice for us once and for all. Next, in order to save humanity from living forever in a fallen condition, God sent the first humans out of the garden. And while this sending contained a mix of protection and punishment, it also included a seed of purpose—*the* purpose of all humanity until Jesus returned.

The word for "send" used here is the Hebrew equivalent of the Greek *apostello*. You might recognize that as the source of our word *apostle*. The Latin word for "send" is *missio*. That's where we get the word *mission*. All of those words mean "to send." And sending is something God loves to do. It is how He reveals Himself to us. It is where we receive our purpose. God is a sending God, a God in mission, a God who takes the risk of extending Himself because of His unfathomable love.

God the Father sent His Word and Spirit for the purpose of creation. He sent Abraham, Moses, and the prophets. "Whom shall I send?" He asked in Isaiah 6:8. And, of course, He sent His only Son to save us.

The sent Son of God continued the sending. He sent His followers into the harvest:

After this the Lord appointed seventy-two others and sent them on ahead of Him, two by two, into every town and place where He Himself was about to go. And He said to them, "The harvest is plentiful, but the laborers are few. Therefore pray earnestly to the Lord of the harvest to send out laborers into His harvest. Go your way; behold, I am sending you." (Luke 10:1–3)

The Holy Spirit was sent to comfort, teach, and counsel: "But when the Helper comes, whom I will send to you from the Father, the Spirit of truth, who proceeds from the Father, He will bear witness about Me" (John 15:26).

Even the victorious Lamb of God on the throne in the Book of Revelation continues to send: "And between the throne and the four living creatures and among the elders I saw a Lamb standing, as though it had been slain, with seven horns and with seven eyes, which are the seven spirits of God sent out into all the earth" (5:6).

God sends.

It's very important to know that God didn't merely expel Adam and Eve from the garden, He *sent* them. Genesis 3:23 says that God sent Adam to "serve" the earth from which he was taken. The word for "serve" is the same word used of Jesus, the Suffering Servant, foretold in Isaiah 42. It is a word used for serving God and serving others. The phrase could imply that Adam was sent to serve the inhabited earth. This verse may very well contain one of God's amazing surprises: that Adam and Eve were the first "apostles," ones sent to make known the grace and love of God.

The form of the verb found in Genesis 3:23 is used at least a half dozen times in the Old Testament for sending, not just for banishing. It is used for purpose, not merely punishment. Of course, in addition to the meaning of the word itself, the sending character of

God that unfolds throughout the Scriptures reinforces this small indication of God's larger purpose for His people. We are sent. We are the shining light of God's grace in the world—the city on a hill and the lamp set high on a stand, so that all who see may give glory to God in heaven (Matthew 5:14–16). This is our high calling. This is the significance we yearn for. This is the life we crave. And God gives it to us as a precious gift.

It happened to Daniel. From Daniel 2:4 through Daniel 7, the Book of Daniel is written in the Aramaic language. This was the language of the world. The whole world would hear the message of the true God in its own language.

Oh, that Henry Dunant would have trusted God's amazing purpose! During Dunant's lowest days, a woman by the name of Clara Barton happened to be visiting Europe for rest after her heroic relief work during the Civil War in the United States. She stopped in Geneva, Switzerland, and read Dunant's account of the battle of Solferino. She even volunteered with members of the International Red Cross to help victims of the Franco-Prussian War in 1870. Barton was inspired by Dunant's compassion and vision. Upon returning to the United States, she worked tirelessly for a congressional charter for the American Red Cross. In 1900, the United States Congress granted the charter for an organization that bears the cross and helps countless numbers of people to this day.

Clara Barton died just two years after Henry Dunant, but instead of dying in bitterness and doubt, Clara Barton died recognizing the amazing purpose of God, the faithful and gracious work of Father, Son, and Holy Spirit—even through the rigors of adversity.[4]

Notes

1. en.wikipedia.org/wiki/Henry_Dunant#Nobel_Peace_ Prize; www.nobelprize.org/nobel_prizes/peace/laure- ates/1901/dunant-bio.html

2. Gustaf Wingren, translated by Carl C. Rasmussen, *Luther on Vocation* (Philadelphia: Muhlenberg Press, 1957), 180, 183.

3. Gerhard Kittel, ed., *Theological Dictionary of the New Testament* (Grand Rapids: Eerdmans, 1968), vol. 4, 704.

4. www.redcross.org/about-us/history/clara-barton

5. Paul McCain, ed., *Concordia: The Lutheran Confessions*, second edition (St. Louis: Concordia Publishing House, 2006), 400–401.

6. McCain, 401–2.

7. McCain, 406.

STUDY GUIDE FOR CHAPTER TWO

YOUR AMAZING PURPOSE

An ancient confession of faith of the Christian Church is called the Apostles' Creed. This creed was drawn from the teaching of those who witnessed Jesus' life, death, and resurrection. It begins, "I believe in God, the Father Almighty, Maker of heaven and earth."

1. As you experience struggles in life, what help and encouragement do you receive from the fact that God is your Creator?

Martin Luther commented:

We ought, therefore, daily to recite this article [God is our creator]. We ought to impress it upon our mind and remember it by all that meets our eyes and by all good that falls to us. Wherever we escape from disaster or danger, we ought to remember that it is God who gives and does all these things. In these escapes we sense and see His fatherly heart and His surpassing love toward us [Exodus 34:6]. In this way the heart would be warmed and kindled to be thankful, and to use all such good things to honor and praise God.[5]

2. Talk about how God remembers you each day—how you have seen God's protection and provision in your life.

3. Read Titus 3:3–8. How do these verses describe God's plan of salvation through Jesus?

The Second Article of the Apostles' Creed confesses faith in Jesus: "And in Jesus Christ, His only Son, our Lord, who was conceived by the Holy Spirit, born of the virgin Mary, suffered under Pontius Pilate, was crucified, died and was buried. He descended into hell. The third day He rose again from the dead. He ascended into heaven and sits at the right hand of God, the Father Almighty. From thence He will come to judge the living and the dead."

Martin Luther commented on this article of faith:

> For when we had been created by God the Father and had received from Him all kinds of good, the devil came and led us into disobedience, sin, death, and all evil [Genesis 3]. So we fell under God's wrath and displeasure and were doomed to eternal damnation, just as we had merited and deserved. There was no counsel, help, or comfort until this only and eternal Son of God—in His immeasurable goodness—had compassion upon our misery and wretchedness. He came from heave to help us [John 1:9]. So those tyrants and jailers are all expelled now. In their place has come Jesus Christ, Lord of life, righteousness, every blessing, and salvation. He has delivered us poor, lost people from hell's jaws, has won us, has made us free [Romans 8:1–2], and has brought us again into the Father's favor and grace. He has taken us as His own property under His shelter and protection [Psalm 61:3–4] so that He may govern us by His righteousness, wisdom, power, life, and blessedness.[6]

4. Discuss the "messes" God has rescued you from, and how God has used struggles in your life for purposes of His good and glory.

The Third Article of the Apostles' Creed refers to the Holy Spirit: "I believe in the Holy Spirit, the holy Christian church, the communion of saints, the forgiveness of sins, the resurrection of the body, and the life everlasting. Amen."

Martin Luther said:

> Now this is the article of the Creed that must always be and remain in use. For we have already received creation. Redemption, too, is finished. But the Holy Spirit carries on His work without ceasing to the Last Day. For that purpose He has appointed a congregation upon earth by which He speaks and does everything. For He has not yet brought together all His Christian Church [*Christenheit*] [John 10:16] or granted all forgiveness.[7]

5. Read 1 Corinthians 6:10–11. Describe what these verses say about the work of the Holy Spirit.

6. Read John 14:25–27 and John 15:26–27. What does Jesus say about the work of the Holy Spirit in your life and the Spirit's impact on your service to others?

7. How does God send you as His servant and ambassador in each area of your life (personal life, family, job, neighborhood, hobbies, volunteer work, etc.)?

8. Read Isaiah 55:10–11. According to these verses, what promise does God give you as you are sent with His Word of truth and life?

9. How does the gathered community of believers—called "the Church"—strengthen you in your knowledge of God and encourage you in your service to Him?

THREE

> "May the God of hope fill you with all joy and peace in believing, so that by the power of the Holy Spirit you may abound in hope."
>
> Romans 15:13

YOUR UNEXPECTED HOPE

DISASTER

Navy SEAL Marcus Luttrell lay on the rocky floor of a dark and cold cave in Afghanistan. He had no food and no weapon. He was suffering from shrapnel wounds, a broken back, and a gunshot wound. Locals had carried him there and left him. It was there he hit a low point. He said, "In the remains of that night, I fell to pieces, finally lost my mind and sobbed hopelessly out of pure fear, offering no further resistance to anything. I thought I could not take it any longer."[1]

Just a short time before this sense of hopelessness hit, Luttrell had been on a special reconnaissance mission with three of his fellow SEALs. On June 27, 2005, Michael Murphy, Danny Dietz, and Matthew Axelson had been covertly inserted into Taliban territory with Luttrell to watch for a notorious Taliban leader. Hours after they moved into position, they accidentally encountered three local goat herders—one was just a teen. Although they knew it would put them in great danger, the SEALs decided to let them go. Before the SEAL team could reach a safe position, they were ambushed by hundreds of armed Taliban fighters. After a heroic firefight, Luttrell's three fellow SEALs were killed. Marcus Luttrell was blown off the side of the mountain as explosives detonated around him. He slid down a steep escarpment and scrambled to find a hiding place. Wounded and battered, hobbling through miles of steep, rocky terrain, he evaded his pursuers. After hours of grueling movement, parched and brokenhearted, Marcus Luttrell collapsed next to a small waterfall. When he raised his head to finally get a drink, he discovered he was staring down the barrel of a rifle.

It would not be a stretch to say that three young men in the Book of Daniel felt the same way. Mishael, Hananiah, and Azariah—also known as Shadrach, Meshach, and Abednego—found themselves staring into a blazing furnace. They, too, were in a foreign land. They, too, were victims of a devious warlord.

It all started when Nebuchadnezzar, the king of Babylon, decided to build a ninety-foot golden image. He may have been inspired to construct this massive figure after he dreamed about the statue that crumbled because of its iron and clay feet. That image perished, but surely a solid-gold statue would last forever—and maybe his kingdom with it! So Nebuchadnezzar commissioned his giant golden figure and invited all of the officials of Babylon to the dedication celebration. After the crowd gathered, a herald proclaimed:

> You are commanded, O peoples, nations, and languages, that when you hear the sound of the horn, pipe, lyre, trigon, harp, bagpipe, and every kind of music, you are to fall down and worship the golden image that King Nebuchadnezzar has set up. And whoever does not fall down and worship shall immediately be cast into a burning fiery furnace. (Daniel 3:4–6)

The king was not the type of person to start with gentle persuasion. So, when the music started, everyone fell down to worship the image of gold—everyone except the Jewish boys who happened to be attending their first image dedication party. It did not take long for some of the king's wise men to let Nebuchadnezzar know that the young outsiders weren't going along with the crowd. In fact, some resentment oozes from their tattling to the king:

> There are certain Jews whom you have appointed over
> the affairs of the province of Babylon: Shadrach, Me-
> shach, and Abednego. These men, O king, pay no at-
> tention to you; they do not serve your gods or worship
> the golden image that you have set up. (v. 12)

Shadrach, Meshach, and Abednego were interlopers who had embarrassed and undermined the king. He was not happy. Nebuchadnezzar didn't try to get friendly with the boys from Jerusalem. Fire was coming out of his ears along with the fire brewing in the furnace:

> Then Nebuchadnezzar in furious rage commanded
> that Shadrach, Meshach, and Abednego be brought.
> So they brought these men before the king. Nebu-
> chadnezzar answered and said to them, "Is it true, O
> Shadrach, Meshach, and Abednego, that you do not
> serve my gods or worship the golden image that I have
> set up? Now if you are ready when you hear the sound
> of the horn, pipe, lyre, trigon, harp, bagpipe, and ev-
> ery kind of music, to fall down and worship the image
> that I have made, well and good. But if you do not
> worship, you shall immediately be cast into a burning

fiery furnace. And who is the god who will deliver you out of my hands?" (vv. 13–15)

If you're familiar with what happened, you can look back and snicker a bit as you see the divine setup happening. But in the moment, the situation looked pretty hopeless. Like Marcus Luttrell, these three young men in a foreign and hostile land were facing certain death. Disaster had struck.

YOUR UNEXPECTED HOPE

I wonder if that's where you're at as you read these words. There are times in life when you feel like there is no way out. More than that, with every fiber of your being and with every thought you muster, you can't envision any possible alternatives to the hopelessness you're experiencing. How can you find a way out when cancer has taken over your insides? How can you imagine an escape after the death of a loved one has laid you low in grief and has carved a cavern of loneliness in your heart? How can you dream of any hope when you've been injured deeply by a cruel and heartless person? How can you adjust your thought process when depression has imprisoned you in a dark cell of sadness? How can you uncover an alternative to the agonizing decision you're facing when all options have been exhausted? How can you get up again after failure or hopelessness has laid you low?

Sometimes, you are truly helpless. Truly stumped. Completely perplexed. Up against a relentless adversary. Out of options and ideas. And it is in those moments when our hope ends that the hope God gives begins.

In the Bible, the word *hope* is used most—about thirty-one

times—in the Psalms. I would have expected that. The Psalms contain stirring songs of praise, sincere pleas for mercy, and strong expressions of trust in God. These biblical songs reflect the many facets of a faith walk with God. The two biblical books that come in tied for second place for their use of the word *hope* are the Book of Romans and the Book of Job. Each uses the word about seventeen times. To be honest, I would have expected Romans. The great missionary and evangelist, Paul, shared the message of the Gospel with strength and passion. He communicated the great message of hope in God's grace and righteousness for believers in Rome. But the Book of Job and *hope*?

Job is a book of disaster and loss. One of the most ancient books of the Bible, it plunges into the mysteries of evil and suffering. It contains the criticism of so-called friends and the despair of a man who can't understand why the world is crashing down upon him. It is a book that showcases human helplessness and pain. And that is why the persistent expression of hope is so unexpected. Job is referring to God when he declares, "Though He slay me, I will hope in Him" (Job 13:15).

The Hebrew word for "hope" contains a sense of expectation, of waiting for dependable help to arrive. Our strength, resources, and ingenuity reach their end, so we wait for God to step in. He is our only hope—even in the face of death. As Marcus Luttrell evaded his enemy, he said, "To be honest, I really thought I might be finished now. I was full of despair, wondering if I might black out, begging God to help me."[2] Over and over again, he recited Psalm 23, the psalm of the SEALs:

The LORD is my shepherd; I shall not want. He makes me lie down in green pastures. He leads me beside still waters. He restores my soul. He leads me in paths of righteousness for His name's sake. Even though I walk through the valley of the shadow of death, I will fear no evil, for You are with me; Your rod and Your staff, they comfort me. You prepare a table before me in the presence of my enemies; You anoint my head with oil; my cup overflows. Surely goodness and mercy shall follow me all the days of my life, and I shall dwell in the house of the LORD forever.

The final word of Psalm 23 is "forever." When the here-and-now fails us, God gives us the gift of forever, the certain hope that the here-and-now is not the end. The apostle Peter faced the wall of personal failure in his relationship with Jesus. Peter fell asleep during Jesus' most agonizing hour in the Garden of Gethsemane. Then, forsaking his teacher and friend, he proceeded three times to deny that he knew Jesus. But Peter was given the gift of hope. He described it this way:

Blessed be the God and Father of our Lord Jesus Christ! According to His great mercy, He has caused us to be born again to a living hope through the resurrection of Jesus Christ from the dead, to an inheritance that is imperishable, undefiled, and unfading, kept in heaven for you. (1 Peter 1:3–4)

Even when the worst happens, you have reason to hope. Even when disaster strikes, you have the eternal hope of God who is living and active. You have the hope of the mighty God who cares about you. You have the living hope of Jesus who defeated the impossible obstacle of death. The apostle Paul, who knew his share of struggles, threats, difficulty, and pain, called the Son of God "Jesus our hope" (1 Timothy 1:1). He knew that even if the here-and-now crumbles, we have the hope of forever. We have that hope because Jesus, our hope, made His way through the rigors of life. He took our pain, guilt, sin, and failure upon Himself and put it to death on the cross. Then, doing what we could never do, He rose from death so that our hope would never end.

The unexpected and miraculous hope of God has been the theme of people whose lives have been reached by God throughout history. It has been the banner raised to all people and nations. When all looks lost, there is still hope. This hope is found in the God of hope. The prophet Isaiah expressed the miracle of God's hope this way:

> Why do you complain, Jacob? Why do you say, Israel, "My way is hidden from the LORD; my cause is disregarded by my God"? Do you not know? Have you not heard? The LORD is the everlasting God, the Creator of the ends of the earth. He will not grow tired or weary, and His understanding no one can fathom. He gives strength to the weary and increases the power of the weak. Even youths grow tired and weary, and young men stumble and fall; *but those who hope in the LORD* will renew their strength. They will soar on wings like eagles; they will run and not grow weary, they will walk and not be faint. (Isaiah 40:27–31 NIV, emphasis added)

HELP

Marcus Luttrell kept praying and reciting Psalm 23 as he crawled on his hands and knees through the mountainous forest. He said, "It was all I had, just a plaintive cry to God who was with me, but whose ways were becoming unclear to me."[3] That's when he found water, and that's when he encountered the men with the rifles. He thought it was the end. He thought he had been defeated. But then the man in front of him lowered his rifle. He shouted, "American! Okay! Okay!"

What unfolded over the ensuing hours and days was a totally surprising turn of events. It was completely unexpected. The man shouting reassurance to Luttrell was named Sarawa, a doctor in a local Afghan village. Sarawa and his Pashtun tribesmen huddled to discuss Marcus Luttrell's fate. In those moments when Luttrell was bleeding and helpless, these local villagers decided to enter into a practice called *lokhay warkawal,* literally meaning "the giving of a pot." It was the practice of hospitality in Pashtunwalai tribal law. But more than simply offering a meal or welcoming a guest, this cultural tradition meant fierce loyalty. In addition to providing care and shelter to a stranger, the entire village would commit to defending their visitor—even if it meant their own deaths. Once decided, the commitment was non-negotiable. Marcus Luttrell was suddenly in the best hands possible.[4]

Shadrach, Meshach, and Abednego would discover the same thing. After the king's threat, the three boys gave a gutsy, faith-filled reply:

> O Nebuchadnezzar, we have no need to answer you in this matter. If this be so, our God whom we serve is able to deliver us from the burning fiery furnace, and

He will deliver us out of your hand, O king. But if not, be it known to you, O king, that we will not serve your gods or worship the golden image that you have set up. (Daniel 3:16–18)

The trio wouldn't budge. They were not going to cave in to the king's demand. They would not sacrifice their integrity or compromise their commitment to the God of heaven. The Bible tells us that after hearing their little speech, King Nebuchadnezzar's attitude and expression changed—but not for the better. Shadrach, Meshach, and Abednego's resistance made Nebuchadnezzar even more furious. He ordered the furnace to be heated seven times hotter than usual. He commanded his strongest men to tie up the three stubborn foreigners and throw them into the flames. The fire was so intense that the men who threw the threesome into the furnace perished from the raging inferno. But as the young men were hurled into what seemed to be certain death, as they closed their eyes and gritted their teeth amidst heat, smoke, and flame, they were, amazingly, in the best hands possible.

You may be at your worst—or think you are—when times look very difficult. But God is always at His best. Even when it seems that He is absent, God is always at His best. We just can't see that all the time. I wonder what Shadrach, Meshach, and Abednego thought when they opened their eyes in the flames and realized they weren't dying. God didn't let them escape or go unnoticed during the dedication of the golden image. He didn't soothe the king's temper. He didn't cause a furnace malfunction. He didn't orchestrate a miraculous escape from the king's mighty men. God allowed His three faithful followers to be bound and thrown into a raging furnace. Sometimes He does the same thing with you or with ones you love. Why? Why the trouble, worry, and stress?

I don't know if there is a single answer to this very big question, but as followers of the Savior, we are signed up for high-risk duty this side of heaven. God may put us in a situation that leads to personal hurt and heartbreak in order to give someone a chance to be reached by Jesus' love. Or God may allow our lives to be broken and hurt so that we have access to people who have experienced the same brokenness and pain. Into dark corners and to people who seem out of reach, the Good News of God's love in Jesus Christ can be delivered. We are instruments in God's hands, redeemed and loved by Him but privileged to share in the sufferings of Jesus. The apostle Paul said, "Now if we are children, then we are heirs—heirs of God and co-heirs with Christ, if indeed we share in His sufferings in order that we may also share in His glory" (Romans 8:17 NIV).

Sometimes, we can see God's reasoning and plan in our lives. There are times when we understand how God grew us or reached others through our adversity. But there are other times when we just don't understand. The flames are fierce, and the circumstances do not make sense.

Only in the midst of the flames did Shadrach, Meshach, and Abednego begin to realize what was happening. Looking through the fire, they saw King Nebuchadnezzar leap to his feet in amazement. The king peered into the furnace and asked his henchmen, *"Did we not cast three men bound into the fire?"* (Daniel 3:24, italics added). The yes-men nodded their heads dutifully. But the king told them, *"But I see four men unbound, walking in the midst of the fire, and they are not hurt; and the appearance of the fourth is like a son of the gods"* (v. 25, italics added). The king called the men to come out of the furnace. Shadrach, Meshach, and Abednego emerged without a scratch or burn. Their clothes were in pristine condition. They didn't even smell like a fire.

Then it started to come together. The three boys from Jerusalem may have begun to understand why in the world they had to endure this frightening trial. God was using them to change the king's heart. God enlisted them in this stressful captivity and put them in a literal furnace so that a godless and straying nation would hear what it needed most: the news of a Savior.

The king saw that the true God was not simply a revealer of mysteries, but one who was more powerful than the strongest fire and more authoritative than the most urgent commands of a strong-willed king. The king realized that the Most High God came to be with His people and was able to save them from the hand of any earthly king. So, to the astonishment of Shadrach, Meshach, and Abednego, the king shared a message with the world that outdid any witness the people of Israel had communicated for the past few hundred years:

> Nebuchadnezzar answered and said, "Blessed be the God of Shadrach, Meshach, and Abednego, who has sent His angel and delivered His servants, who trusted in Him, and set aside the king's command, and yielded up their bodies rather than serve and worship any god except their own God. Therefore I make a decree: Any people, nation, or language that speaks anything against the God of Shadrach, Meshach, and Abednego shall be torn limb from limb, and their houses laid in ruins, for there is no other god who is able to rescue in this way." (vv. 28–29)

It wasn't exactly a message that would be recommended by the church evangelism committee. Being torn limb from limb and having your house laid in ruins was a little strong, but the beauty of the message is seen in its rawness. Nebuchadnezzar was being drawn closer to God. He was seeing that God provided a different kind of life that was pretty amazing. It was a life that was selfless, courageous, and admirable. It was a life that couldn't even be fouled up by the strongest forces on earth. It was a life that was close to God. This is something Nebuchadnezzar craved. Having a cadre of enchanters, magicians, and diviners gave evidence to the fact that Nebuchadnezzar wanted to connect with the divine. The king's agonizing deliberation over dreams proved that he had a deep desire for more than just what this life offered. To see how God had helped Shadrach, Meshach, and Abednego showed that the Most High God had the remarkable inclination to defend His people even in the face of death.

It's the ultimate *lokhay warkawal*. And it's what God chose for you. When He sent His only Son to die so you could be spared from the consequences of your sin, He claimed you as His welcomed guest. More than that, He claimed you as His own child. St. Paul announced, "But now in Christ Jesus you who once were far off have been brought near by the blood of Christ" (Ephesians 2:13). John declared, "See what kind of love the Father has given to us, that we should be called children of God; and so we are" (1 John 3:1).

This kindness and welcome, this unique life, is what we crave. And it's all about God's grace. Jesus steps forward as your advocate. He speaks for you and defends you. John said, "My little children, I am writing these things to you so that you may not sin. But if anyone does sin, we have an advocate with the Father, Jesus Christ the righteous" (1 John 2:1).

I remember looking for a summer job during college. Jobs that paid more than minimum wage were not easy to come by. It was then I discovered the importance of the phrase "It's not *what* you know; it's *who* you know." The only way I was going to get a decent-paying job was to have a relationship with someone who was connected. That's where my dad came in. He worked for a drugstore chain that was connected to a grocery store company. He heard about grocery warehouse jobs that offered a good wage. After doing some checking and finding the right person to talk to, I had an open door to apply—and apply I did! I got the job and kept it every summer. My two college co-workers over the summer also had family connections. It helped to have an advocate.

As I look at my life, I see God's grace at every turn. I see His advocacy in the way He formed my faith, in the way He shaped me through some difficult years growing up, in the way He led me to a college and a career, in the way He connected me with my wife, and in the way He shapes and forms me to this day. I couldn't have planned any of God's blessings—and I don't deserve His goodness and help, but His grace prevails. What a humbling gift!

Shadrach, Meshach, and Abednego were given the opportunity to sit in the company of the king. More than that, they were able to introduce Nebuchadnezzar to the God of heaven. Who could have planned such a course for their lives?

As the now-cleaned-up, freshly clothed, patched-up, hidden, and defended Marcus Luttrell lay safely on the dirt floor of a house in Sabray, an Afghan village, he was amazed at the turn of events and at the new hope he had. A struggle still loomed, but suddenly, another chance at life was unfolding—all because of grace.

> And we rejoice in the hope of the glory of God. Not
> only so, but we also rejoice in our sufferings, because
> we know that suffering produces perseverance; per-
> severance, character; and character, hope. And hope
> does not disappoint us, because God has poured out
> His love into our hearts by the Holy Spirit, whom He
> has given us. (Romans 5:2–5 NIV)

Hope from God never disappoints. It always involves a gracious miracle—either on this side of the furnace or the other. His
help is certain. His rescue allows us to live a bold, gutsy, uncommon life—one of certainty that He will come through and that His
grace will prevail.

A LIFE OF FREEDOM

Of course, one of the greatest episodes of rescue and freedom
is one that almost never happened—at least from our earthly point
of view. It started in ancient Egypt, where the people of Israel had
made their home since the time of Joseph. After Joseph and his
generation died, the new king of Egypt became nervous about the
foreigners who dominated the population. In order to prevent an
uprising, the new king put slave masters over the Israelites. He also
implemented a policy of killing every Hebrew baby boy. Fear led
to oppression and cruelty. God's people were plunged into a miserable existence under ever-increasing tyranny.

Many years before, God had told Abraham this terrible time
would come. When God promised Abraham a prosperous nation
that would bless many, He told Abraham, "Know for certain that

your offspring will be sojourners in a land that is not theirs and will be servants there, and they will be afflicted for four hundred years" (Genesis 15:13). It was dreadful news that came to fruition in the land of Egypt.

If you've seen Cecil B. DeMille's *The Ten Commandments*, or if you've watched the animated feature *The Prince of Egypt*, you can visualize what happened. Moses was secretly saved from the Egyptian king's infanticide by being placed in a basket in the Nile River. The king's daughter found the baby, named him Moses, and raised him as her own. But life was not smooth sailing for Moses. Being raised as an Egyptian while knowing his Hebrew lineage created dissonance in his heart. Exodus 2 tells us:

> One day, when Moses had grown up, he went out to his people and looked on their burdens, and he saw an Egyptian beating a Hebrew, one of his people. He looked this way and that, and seeing no one, he struck down the Egyptian and hid him in the sand. (vv. 11–12)

This outburst didn't work out very well. Moses ended up being scorned by his own people and becoming a hunted murderer in Egypt. He fled the country and went into hiding in the desert. God had chosen Moses as the deliverer of His people, but Moses decided to implement his own plan. It backfired. Nobody would listen to him now. He had fallen out of favor with the Egyptians. His own people would never follow him. He went from prince to fugitive, from liberator to shepherd. He was unknown and unwanted. He experienced a sentence of solitary confinement in the wilderness of Midian for forty years.

That's enough to make you lose hope. In fact, you may feel just like Moses. Sometimes you wonder if you've fouled up God's plan for your life. You start to believe that you're no longer any use to Him or that you're settling for the cut-rate, discount plan for your life. Because of a decision you've made or an impulsive action, you feel cast aside or disqualified.

Moses may have felt that way during his forty-year layoff. True, he was able to settle down, get married, and start a family. God's grace still prevailed in his life. But he may have believed that he had squandered any chance to help his people out of their torment and distress. He may have been convinced that while God was being kind, He had removed any chance for Moses to fulfill the purpose he was most passionate about.

Fortunately, God doesn't think that way. The Bible says, "But God shows His love for us in that while we were still sinners, Christ died for us" (Romans 5:8). The God of unexpected hope does miraculous things to free us from our prisons and give us new life. He'll even change history.

Yes, God changed history for Moses. Acts 7:23 tells us that Moses was forty years old when he killed the Egyptian. Exodus 7:7 lets us know that Moses was eighty years old when he began to speak with Pharaoh, the Egyptian king. Exodus 12:40–41 says, "The time that the people of Israel lived in Egypt was 430 years. At the end of 430 years, on that very day, all the hosts of the LORD went out from the land of Egypt." What does all this add up to? God's grace. You see, if the people of Israel were going to be released on schedule after 400 years, Moses would have been activated as the deliverer when he was fifty years old. But because Moses sprang into action ten years early, God graciously waited. He patiently walked with Moses, preparing him, restoring him, and setting things right in Egypt. Two important events happened while Moses was in hiding.

Exodus 2:23 tells us, "During those many days the king of Egypt died, and the people of Israel groaned because of their slavery and cried out for help. Their cry for rescue from slavery came up to God." Exodus 4:19 says, "And the LORD said to Moses in Midian, 'Go back to Egypt, for all the men who were seeking your life are dead.'"

After forty years, the threat was gone. The need intensified. The suspicion waned. God did the unexpected. He delayed the release of His people by thirty years so He could restore Moses and renew his hope. Before the people of Israel were freed with great signs and wonders, Moses experienced an exodus from the prison of guilt, shame, and unworthiness. If you read the complete account of Moses' call in Exodus 3–4, you can hear God walking Moses through all his doubts. Stuttering? God would provide Aaron. Uncertainty about what to say? God gave Moses the words. A fear of unbelief? God gave Moses miraculous signs. Feeling like he was just an unworthy shepherd, the occupation most scorned by the Egyptians? Moses' shepherd's staff became the miraculous "staff of God" (Exodus 4:20).

Would God do anything less to show His grace to you and to give you hope? The answer to that question is in His Son, Jesus, sent to rewrite your history with the forgiveness of sins. And, as Paul declared:

> Do you not know that all of us who have been baptized into Christ Jesus were baptized into His death? We were buried therefore with Him by baptism into death, in order that, just as Christ was raised from the dead by the glory of the Father, we too might walk in newness of life. (Romans 6:3–4)

New life. It's God's specialty. New life is what God gave the liberated Hebrew slaves after they miraculously exited Egypt. Gathered around Mount Sinai, the people waited as God visited them and spoke to them. God wasn't simply going to turn the newly freed people loose in the desert. He wanted them to have a full life. So He stopped to teach them. In Exodus 20, we hear God speak what we call the Ten Commandments. Unfortunately, the Ten Commandments have a reputation for being the "have-no-fun" and "tow-the-line-or-else" strict Law of God. That wasn't the intent or the context at all. These ten words from God were words of new life.

Think about what the people of Israel had gone through. After 430 years in slavery, all they knew was a life of oppression:

❋ Go to the market and choose a few goodies for the family? No. Eat the slave rations when and where the taskmasters say.

❋ Hang out with friends and converse until the stars brightly light the sky? No. Ration sleep as you try to meet the king's deadline for the latest project.

❋ Worship freely and grow as followers of the God of Abraham, Isaac, and Jacob? No. Secretly hang on to the vestiges of your ancestral faith, while having the gods of Egypt forced on your family.

❋ Grow in personal learning and spiritual discipline? No. Have your life scheduled and orchestrated by the overlords of the Egyptian dynasty.

❋ Enjoy a social network of friendship and respect? No. Live under the abusive treatment of slave drivers and see life cheapened and disrespected every day.

After 430 years, the people had no life! They forgot how to worship, how to conduct themselves with one another, and how to trust that anyone was looking out for them. They didn't know what it was like to be content with what they had or to serve one another generously. So God gave them a precious gift. Along with physical freedom, He gave them spiritual and emotional freedom. He gave them a life! It was a welcome gift. Exodus 20 begins with the recollection of miraculous deliverance from bondage, as God said, "I am the LORD your God, who brought you out of the land of Egypt, out of the house of slavery" (v. 2). Then He unfolded a beautiful life before them:

> You shall have no other gods before Me. . . . You shall not take the name of the LORD your God in vain. . . . Remember the Sabbath day, to keep it holy. . . . Honor your father and your mother, that your days may be long in the land that the LORD your God is giving you. You shall not murder. You shall not commit adultery. You shall not steal. You shall not bear false witness against your neighbor. You shall not covet your neighbor's house; you shall not covet your neighbor's wife, or his male servant, or his female servant, or his ox, or his donkey, or anything that is your neighbor's. (Exodus 20:3, 7–8, 12–17)

God gave His people the life they craved: a relationship with Him, a healthy rhythm for life, the foundation for family and social relationships, respect for life, honor in sexuality and marriage, a balanced approach to possessions and reputation, and the blessings of contentment and gratitude.

I remember teaching the Ten Commandments to junior high

kids. I asked them, "Do you want to have friends and be popular?" Every one of them wanted both! That's when I directed them to the Ten Commandments. Instead of a junior high life of selfishness, unkindness, bullying, putting others down, and feeling empty because you don't have the latest stuff like other people do, God opens the door to a life that is good, a life that really works. Those junior high students could be the people who were confident and kind, who befriended others, and who knew what was really important in life. Suddenly, people would want to be with them and want to be like them. Of course, following God's ways may not lead to popularity at all. It may lead to persecution. But as the Bible says, "Love never fails" (1 Corinthians 13:8 NIV). The life of loving God and loving others was a gift from God that was worth the risk and worth the witness. God's gift of life brought balance, purity, love, and emotional fulfillment to lives wrecked by slavery.

The question I was asking those junior high students was this: "Who will set the agenda for your life?" Would they let the world, the devil, or their own sinful flesh be their taskmasters? Or would they live in freedom?

The freedom of life in Jesus Christ means that you are raised to life and given a life. Being a rescued and liberated child of God doesn't mean that you are saved and then you have to cobble a life together under your own power. Following and trusting in Jesus doesn't mean that you're freed from sin and death so you can figure life out on your own. No, God gives the whole package. In a world of addiction, bad influences, peer pressure, depression, grief, disheartening jobs, family strife, money issues, war, political infighting, church infighting, fatigue, sexual corruption, and much more, God provides us with life that is good. It's the freedom we crave.

Hope upon Hope

After five tense days in the Afghan village, Marcus Luttrell was rescued by a team of Army Rangers. While the U.S. military identified a rescue beacon Luttrell activated in the village, they couldn't be sure it was one of the Navy SEALs. What made them certain was the action of the village elder. After considering all possible options to get Marcus out, the elder of the village decided that the only path to freedom was to walk forty miles over mountainous territory to the U.S. military base. Marcus was too injured to travel that far, so the elder made the trip himself. He walked forty miles through dangerous territory to rescue a stranger.

God chose a similar path. He sent His Son into a hostile and sinful world to rescue us. Like Marcus Luttrell, we received the gift of unexpected hope and new life. We were surprised with absolute grace.

The apostle Paul said, "For freedom Christ has set us free; stand firm therefore, and do not submit again to a yoke of slavery" (Galatians 5:1). The liberating work of Jesus on the cross has given us unexpected hope that lasts forever. It's a story worth telling and a life worth living.

Notes

1. Marcus Luttrell, *Lone Survivor* (New York: Little, Brown and Company, 2007), 300.
2. Luttrell, 266.
3. Luttrell, 267.
4. Luttrell, 285–86.
5. Paul McCain, ed., *Concordia: The Lutheran Confessions*, second edition (St. Louis: Concordia Publishing House, 2006), 373.

STUDY GUIDE FOR CHAPTER THREE

YOUR UNEXPECTED HOPE

1. The First Commandment is "You shall have no other gods" (Exodus 20:3). How do life's "furnaces" test who or what your god really is?

2. Read 1 Peter 1:3–4. Why are these words especially significant coming from the apostle Peter?

3. How do these words describe the essence of the Christian life?

4. The Second and Third Commandments describe our relationship with God: "You shall not take the name of the LORD your God in vain" (Exodus 20:7) and "Remember the Sabbath day, to keep it holy" (v. 8). Discuss some practical ways that this direction from God shapes your day-to-day life of faith.

The Fourth Commandment addresses family and leaders: "Honor your father and your mother, that your days may be long in the land that the LORD your God is giving you" (Exodus 20:12). Martin Luther said, "For God has assigned parenthood the highest place. Yes, He has set it up in His own place upon the earth."[5]

5. Read Ephesians 5:21–6:4. What are some key characteristics of a Christian family?

Commandments 5–8 cover the way we treat others: "You shall

not murder. You shall not commit adultery. You shall not steal. You shall not bear false witness against your neighbor" (Exodus 20:13–16).

6. What are some major current cultural struggles these commandments address? Discuss the world's point of view and God's.

7. How do these commandments guide you in your walk with your Savior?

The final two commandments talk about contentment: "You shall not covet your neighbor's house; you shall not covet your neighbor's wife, or his male servant, or his female servant, or his ox, or his donkey, or anything that is your neighbor's" (Exodus 20:17).

8. Read Philippians 4:10–13. What is the apostle Paul saying in these verses about the secret to true contentment?

9. How does your personal contentment develop, and how does it provide a witness of true hope in Jesus Christ to the world?

FOUR

> "Then the LORD said, 'I have surely seen the affliction of My people who are in Egypt and have heard their cry because of their taskmasters. I know their sufferings, and I have come down to deliver them.'" Exodus 3:7–8

YOUR ANSWER TO PRAYER

ACCESS

I'll never forget the day I met one of my childhood radio broadcasting idols. He was standing on his front stoop, wearing a baseball hat, wrinkled jeans, an oversized jacket, and loosely laced tennis shoes. He was smoking a cigarette. All of this was happening across the street from the church I was serving as pastor. The small mission church in Palatine, Illinois, began around the same time my broadcasting idol was at the height of his career on WCFL, Chicago's top-forty rock music leader. Before I arrived on the scene, he used to make wisecracks on the air about the dandelions growing in the church's front lawn. Apparently, the seeds were blowing into his yard—not a good thing. He didn't like weeds in his well-manicured grass. He rode the wave of being a top "shock jock" in radio until the fickle station owners decided that easy listening would be the new format. He complied for a short time until his contract was bought out and he retired.

Now he was our neighbor. His kind and lovely wife was a member of our church, so, as I visited church members during my first year there, I asked if I could pay a visit. That visit started a long and meaningful friendship with a man I once had known only through the speaker of my radio. While I was in grade school, I heard him play the latest hits. During high school, I listened to him while I sat in my room and studied for final exams. And now I sat in his living room, hearing about the amazing life he had lived. At first, he was guarded and a little suspicious. This is a man who lived in the public eye, who was scrutinized by the press and pursued by fans. But after our first visit, he wanted to get together again. He was a deep thinker—a philosopher of sorts whose life experiences led him to ask profound questions about life and God. So we met and talked. We exchanged books. I was privileged to hear about his life, the experiences that meant the most to him, and the times that broke his heart. After he had a serious health scare, we got together more often. The person I knew as a rock DJ and wild public figure became someone I knew as a caring family man who wondered if the institutional church had room for someone like him, but who craved insight into God's mind and heart.

After some building improvements at our church, I would see him watering our new trees along the parkway across the street from his home. He would say to me, "Got to make sure the trees don't die, Rev." That's what he called me: "Rev," with his deep resonant voice. Over those years, I discovered that he cared about creation, he respected God, and he resembled the father in Mark 9 who said, "I believe; help my unbelief!" (v. 24). So we took the journey of faith together. When I first met my DJ idol, I couldn't believe that I had access to this well-known person from my childhood. When I got to know him, I was moved to realize that God brought us together so we could celebrate the access we had together to our heavenly Father.

Think about it: we have access to God. There's no need to clamor for His autograph as He leaves an exclusive club. You don't have to search for covert stories about Him on the Internet. You're not required to buy a gossip magazine to get the latest information about Him. He's not living behind walls and gates in an exclusive Hollywood neighborhood. The Bible says:

> Do not say in your heart, "Who will ascend into heaven?" (that is, to bring Christ down) or "Who will descend into the abyss?" (that is, to bring Christ up from the dead). But what does [the righteousness based on faith] say? "The word is near you, in your mouth and in your heart." (Romans 10:6–8)

Jesus is close. God is accessible. In fact, He invites us to get in touch with Him. In Psalm 50:15, we hear God say, "Call upon Me in the day of trouble; I will deliver you, and you shall glorify Me."

Calling on my DJ neighbor meant making a phone call or ringing his doorbell. Calling on God means talking to Him in prayer. It is access to the Creator of the universe, to the Miracle Worker who rose from the dead, and to the Encourager and Comforter for our lives—simply by talking to Him anytime and anywhere. Prayer is a gift. And it is a gift we crave.

Jesus' disciples craved this miraculous access to God. The Gospel writer Luke tells us, "Now Jesus was praying in a certain place, and when He finished, one of His disciples said to Him, 'Lord, teach us to pray, as John taught his disciples'" (Luke 11:1). Jesus didn't respond by saying, "You're too unworthy to talk directly to the Man Upstairs." He didn't tell His disciples, "You can't just talk to God. You need to attain a certain level of success before you can hobnob with the Big Guy." No. There were no requirements, no prerequisites, no hoops to jump through, and no eligibility standards. Jesus answered this audacious request for complete access to God by saying, "When you pray, say: 'Father, hallowed be Your name'" (Luke 11:2).

Jesus gave complete access to God in the context of a personal and loving relationship. No one had to start a prayer by saying, "I know I shouldn't be talking to You and You probably hate the sound of my unworthy voice." No one had to approach God and say, "This is probably a dumb question, and I know You have much more important things to do." No one had to preface a petition to God with "I understand You're very busy and may not be able to squeeze me in today." Instead, Jesus gave a precious gift. He opened the door to 24/7/365 contact with the almighty and holy God. He framed our relationship with Him in the context of children who have a kind and loving Daddy. In order to get His attention, to have Him listen to our voices and hear the cries of our hearts, we simply say "Father."

HELP, PLEASE

But that's not always easy for us. When my children were little, we taught them to ask us for help anytime they needed it. When trouble came or when sadness swooped in, all they had to do was ask for help. We wanted to do everything we could to provide guidance, consolation, and support. But, if you're a parent, you know it isn't this simple. Instead of hearing, "Daddy, can you help me untangle my Barbie clothes?" I would sometimes see a Barbie doll being tugged on and dropped to the floor in frustration. Instead of being approached with a request for help when a crayon broke, I would, at times, hear a cry of despair and see a sweet daughter give up on coloring a picture. When she was a toddler, one of our daughters used to run away and hide when she hurt herself. This got a little scary. Why not just come to us for help? Why not simply call our name?

But our sinful pride is so strong. Our tendency toward self-sufficiency is powerful. Too often, we would rather spend hours in agony than utter the simple phrase "Help, please." Just ask any husband who refuses to ask for directions and any wife who has spent unnecessary hours in the car, searching for a destination, even with the help of a GPS! We're stubborn, and we like to do life ourselves. We want to solve it, fix it, figure it out, and handle it. We don't want to appear weak by leaning on God.

That was King Nebuchadnezzar's problem. He was a typical, headstrong, stubborn, do-it-yourself kind of leader. True, the God of heaven could overrule a fiery furnace. Yes, the Most High God could reveal mysteries. But when crunch time came, the king was going to rely on himself. God might be good for a few isolated situations and for some religious types—like Daniel and his buddies—but when it came down to real life, the king had to take charge. And it was at that point in a life that wavered on the edge of faith and unfaith that Nebuchadnezzar had another mysterious dream:

> I, Nebuchadnezzar, was at ease in my house and prospering in my palace. I saw a dream that made me afraid. As I lay in bed the fancies and the visions of my head alarmed me. (Daniel 4:4–5)

Just as the king got comfortable with his prosperity and power, panic overwhelmed him. When Nebuchadnezzar started to believe that the world was his oyster and he would use his strength to take whatever he wanted, fear made him feel helpless. The king dreamed about an enormous tree that stretched to the sky. It had beautiful fruit and healthy leaves, and it provided shelter for a variety of living creatures. Suddenly, a holy one from heaven made the proclamation that the tree was to be cut down. Its branches were to be stripped bare, and all the living creatures that sought safety and nourishment from it were to be scattered. Only its stump and roots were to remain, bound by a band of iron and bronze.

Then the stump took on a personal quality. The "holy one's" proclamation declared that he would be wet with the dew of heaven and find company with the beasts of the earth. His mind would be changed from a human's to an animal's. This development would last for seven periods of time. Why? Nebuchadnezzar recounted the purpose declared by the "watchers" and "holy ones" of heaven:

> The sentence is by the decree of the watchers, the decision by the word of the holy ones, to the end that the living may know that the Most High rules the kingdom of men and gives it to whom He will and sets over it the lowliest of men. (Daniel 4:17)

The Most High God was getting personal with Nebuchadnezzar. The Father in heaven was disciplining a stubborn child. God was teaching the king a lesson about who was truly lofty and who was truly lowly. The Lord was trying to show this pagan leader that his life was not a self-constructed achievement, but a gift from Him. Most of all, God was working to draw Nebuchadnezzar close to Him. That's what a loving father does. As Proverbs 3:11–12 says, "My son, do not despise the LORD's discipline or be weary of His reproof, for the LORD reproves him whom He loves, as a father the son in whom he delights."

Nebuchadnezzar showed some humility when he asked Daniel

for help and acknowledged the Spirit of God in him. He told his prized wise man, "This dream I, King Nebuchadnezzar, saw. And you, O Belteshazzar, tell me the interpretation, because all the wise men of my kingdom are not able to make known to me the interpretation, but you are able, for the spirit of the holy gods is in you" (Daniel 4:18).

Daniel understood the dream immediately, but he hesitated before sharing the meaning with the king. After the king coaxed him, Daniel broke the difficult news: The tree was the king in all of his power and dominion. But now God had decreed that the king needed to learn something more about the true God of heaven. Daniel told Nebuchadnezzar:

> You shall be driven from among men, and your dwelling shall be with the beasts of the field. You shall be made to eat grass like an ox, and you shall be wet with the dew of heaven, and seven periods of time shall pass over you, till you know that the Most High rules the kingdom of men and gives it to whom He will. And as it was commanded to leave the stump of the roots of the tree, your kingdom shall be confirmed for you from the time that you know that Heaven rules." (vv. 25–26)

Daniel went on to plead with the king, "Therefore, O king, let my counsel be acceptable to you: break off your sins by practicing righteousness, and your iniquities by showing mercy to the oppressed, that there may perhaps be a lengthening of your prosperity" (v. 27).

Apparently, King Nebuchadnezzar was living an arrogant and selfish life. It's a trap any of us can fall into. Rich or poor, strong or weak, each of us can easily overestimate our own importance. It shows itself in the way we treat others. It can be seen in our refusal to ask for help or to share responsibilities. It is on display when we lift ourselves up by putting others down. Inflated self-importance can cause a businessperson to veer into dishonesty, a politician to make an alliance with corruption, and a Christian to forsake a spirit of service and sacrifice. Arrogance can erect walls of self-sufficiency that shut out the very reason for a person's, company's, or church's existence. Arrogance kills mission and opposes the Spirit of God.

That is the dangerous territory Nebuchadnezzar was in. But despite Daniel's warning, the king refused to change. One year passed. While the king was walking on the rooftop of his palace, he said, "Is not this great Babylon, which I have built by my mighty power as a royal residence and for the glory of my majesty?" (Daniel 4:30). Immediately, we're told, while the king was still speaking, a voice from heaven announced his fate, and he was struck down. He lived in insanity, like an animal, for seven years. Everything was taken away from him until he was humble enough to ask for help. Daniel 4:34 says, "At the end of the days I, Nebuchadnezzar, lifted my eyes to heaven, and my reason returned to me, and I blessed the Most High, and praised and honored Him who lives forever."

The king "lifted [his] eyes to heaven." What is a person doing when he lifts his eyes to heaven? Psalm 121:1–2 gives us an answer: "I lift up my eyes to the hills. From where does my help come? My help comes from the LORD, who made heaven and earth." "Lifting eyes to heaven" means looking for help. Nebuchadnezzar said to God, "Help, please." And God restored him.

That is the last picture we have of King Nebuchadnezzar,

mighty ruler of Babylon. He lifted up his eyes to heaven. He prayed to a gracious Father. And to the whole Babylonian kingdom, Nebuchadnezzar gave a final testimony: "Now I, Nebuchadnezzar, praise and extol and honor the King of heaven, for all His works are right and His ways are just; and those who walk in pride He is able to humble" (Daniel 4:37).

Perhaps Nebuchadnezzar inspired many people in Babylon and beyond to lift their eyes to heaven and say, "Help, please." Perhaps he's even inspired you to do the same. It's a gracious start to the gift of prayer. But how do you keep praying? How do you actively communicate with the God who loves you and gave His life for you?

How to Pray: Your Will Be Done

Jesus' prayer instructions continued: "Your kingdom come, Your will be done, on earth as it is in heaven" (Matthew 6:10). *Your* kingdom come. *Your* will be done. Clearly, we're not the ones calling the shots or charting the course. As King Nebuchadnezzar discovered, a life with God means submitting to His plan. Communication with God involves a humble spirit. Prayer isn't about glorifying yourself. It's about exalting a mighty and gracious Savior.

Not too long ago, I was listening to a New York professional basketball player speak at a press conference. His team had lost again—the tenth loss in a row. He hung his head and said to the room full of reporters, "Pray for us. Seriously. Pray for us."

This man was humbled. He was desperate. His team had experienced one injury after another. No longer was this player dreaming of his hour of glory. He knew he needed help. He and his team needed God's help. This player may have had dreams of superstardom and success, the upwardly mobile climb that earns the accolades of the world. But now he had discovered the humble pathway of downward mobility, the life that understands its dependence on someone much greater.

One day when I was a young pastor, I drove past one of our church member's homes in our neighborhood. The church member commented to her neighbor, who happened to be standing in the yard next to her, "That's my pastor." The neighbor, who had seen me drive by before, replied, "Oh, I thought he was just a yuppie."

You remember what a *yuppie* is, don't you? "Young urban professional," and we could also think of it as "young upwardly mobile professional." When I started my ministry, yuppies were taking society by storm. "Yuppie" described a person who was on the pathway to success. It was a label for someone who was making the professional climb to the top. Although the term isn't used anymore, the climb is still happening. Upward mobility is still a major battle cry. Whether it's manifested in a new SUV, a kid's trendy birthday party, the latest cell phone, or the designer purse, we are tempted with the desire to show the world that we're climbing the ladder of success.

A funny thing happened to my wife and me as we were experiencing this pressure to be upwardly mobile. We had kids. Friends of ours were starting families too. Suddenly, it seemed foolish to talk about success when you were wiping spit-up off your suit coat shoulder, had the smell of baby wipes on your hands, were nodding off because of sleep lost to early morning feedings, and had your financial focus directed at how good a price you could find for a case of formula. In an instant, we were no longer the boss.

An eight-pound, twenty-one-inch, crying, wetting, and eating machine was running the universe! We were simply servants.

What I discovered, and what anyone who cares for another person discovers, is the amazing pathway of *downward mobility*. It means asking "What can I give?" instead of "What can I get?" And it is not a natural inclination. Jesus said, "If anyone would come after Me, let him deny himself and take up his cross and follow Me. For whoever would save his life will lose it, but whoever loses his life for My sake and the gospel's will save it" (Mark 8:34–35). Following Jesus means denying self. It means the sacrifice of your plan for His plan. It means losing your life to gain the life He gives. It means downward mobility. And that is a key component of prayer. When you pray, you acknowledge that you are not in control. When you talk to God, you are ceding control to Him. You enter into an intimate and submissive relationship. You say, "I need You. I need Your help. I need You to listen. I am not the boss." Prayer is undergirded by the belief and commitment that your life is not the center of the universe. There is a bigger picture. When you take the plunge into prayer, you enter the pathway of downward mobility. You bring your vulnerabilities, your fears, and your sins out of hiding and into the light of Jesus Christ because you believe and trust that He can bring healing and restoration.

Maybe that's why prayer is sometimes difficult. As Paul said in Romans 12, you're not thinking of yourself more highly than you ought. But this downward mobility leading into prayer doesn't mean you are a weakling. It doesn't mean you're passive. It means that you tenaciously follow Jesus Christ because you know that in Him there is an answer, in Him there is strength, and in Him there is life.

In Mark 8, Peter was not focusing on humility or downward mobility. He wanted to work *his* plan. He was intent on upward mobility—doing it all himself. And that can happen in your walk with God too. You have a plan. You want your life to unfold in a certain way. So you tell God, "This is how it's supposed to be! And don't mess up my plan!"

But Jesus said to Peter, "Get behind Me, Satan! For you are not setting your mind on the things of God, but on the things of man" (Mark 8:33). God has a different priority. His plan is about the downward mobility of the cross and the ultimate gift of forgiveness and eternal life for His beloved children. Jesus described God's will when He taught the disciples that "the Son of Man must suffer many things and be rejected by the elders and the chief priests and the scribes and be killed, and after three days rise again" (v. 31). Prayer is asking God that this will of salvation be given first priority. It means bringing all your impossibilities to the One who did the impossible for you. It means bringing your sins and failures to the One who took them upon Himself and paid the price for them. It means bringing your old and worn-out life and attitude to the One who makes you a new creation. Prayer is even about bringing death and sadness to the One who defeated death. God sets the pace. Humbly, we trust Him and say, "Your kingdom come, Your will be done, on earth as it is in heaven" (Matthew 6:10).

HOW TO PRAY: ASK

As Jesus taught His disciples how to pray, He continued His instruction by letting them know they could say, "Give us this day our daily bread" (Matthew 6:11). Prayer includes asking for things. In His grace, God wants us to make requests.

During my seminary years, one of the jobs I had was with a landscaping company. A co-worker of mine came in one morning and said, "I got another raise." I had been beating myself up all summer, working hard, going the extra mile, and doing quality work, but I didn't get a raise. So I asked him, "How did you get a raise?" He looked at me and said, "I asked for one." Where do you think I was at the end of the week? *Asking.* And I got the raise.

What if you go through your life with God and never ask Him about the pressing issues and needs you are facing? In His teaching about prayer, Jesus said, "Ask, and it will be given to you; seek, and you will find; knock, and it will be opened to you" (Matthew 7:7–8). But what if you never ask? What if you make the decision *not* to ask God about matters in your life because you feel that you shouldn't bother Him? How can I ever ask God about this? you might think. It's too small and insignificant. And who am I to ask *Him* for some small thing in my life?

Lots of things get in the way of bringing your requests to God. Sometimes, you get into the habit of doing everything yourself. When exhaustion sets in, you may find yourself saying, "Wait a minute. I'd better pray about this." But it's easy to be stubborn, go it alone, and not ask God. There are other times you don't ask God because you get discouraged and tired. You become weary. Things look hopeless. You say to yourself, "Why even pray? I've tried it before. Why try again?" Getting discouraged and worn down can keep you from asking God.

But the Bible says, "You do not have, because you do not ask" (James 4:2). God makes it clear that He is here to help you. "Give us today our daily bread," Jesus taught. Every basic need is in God's care. Nothing is too small. God wants to hear from you. He wants you to ask.

Your Answer to Prayer

When I heard about my fellow landscaper's raise, I was inspired to get into action. I needed that raise. My wife and I were newly married and struggling to get by financially. We had to use spare change to buy gas for the car. We rationed milk. Maybe I felt stubborn and self-sufficient at times. Maybe I got discouraged when nothing was happening. But there's nothing like a little old-fashioned *desperate need* to get some asking going. And who better to go to when you're lonely, when you need a focus in life, when you are experiencing strife in your family, when you encounter tough issues and temptations, when you need help in friendships, or when you deal with money or car troubles? Who better can you go to than God Himself? And why not, when He invites you to come to Him even with the basic and ordinary need of daily bread? Go ahead and ask. Bring every detail to the Power over the problem, the Giver of all goodness, the listening Lord, your faithful Friend. Then, watch what happens.

How to Pray: Watch

Yes, that's the next step in prayer: watch. When I was taught about prayer, I was taught to talk. We were to bring praise, confession of our sins, thanksgiving, and requests to God. But no one ever told me to watch for answers. When I read Psalm 5, I realized that God wanted us to be attentive to His response to our prayers. Verse 3 says, "In the morning, O Lord, You hear my voice; in the morning I lay my requests before You and wait expectantly" (Psalm 5:3 NIV). The English Standard Version of the Bible translates the last line this way: "In the morning I prepare a sacrifice for You and watch." God promises to answer our prayers. It makes sense that we should pay attention, that we should watch and wait in expectation.

Jesus said to His disciples, "And whatever you ask in prayer, you will receive, if you have faith" (Matthew 21:22). And 1 John 5:14–15 says, "And this is the confidence that we have toward Him, that if we ask anything according to His will He hears us. And if we know that He hears us in whatever we ask, we know that we have the requests that we have asked of Him." God makes a commitment to answer prayer. But how do you watch? How do you listen for answers?

Part of watching for God's responses to prayer is making sure clutter is removed from your life. One of the things that may get in the way of seeing God's responses to your prayers is unconfessed sin. The Bible says, "If we say we have not sinned, we make [God] a liar, and His word is not in us" (1 John 1:10). If you are living apart from the will of God, you're keeping Him at a distance. How can you listen to God and watch for His action when you are pushing Him away? Another obstacle to seeing God's responses to your prayers is unforgiveness. In Jesus' discussion about prayer, He taught His disciples to say, "And forgive us our debts, as we also have forgiven our debtors" (Matthew 6:12). It is not uncommon to be blinded by bitterness or preoccupied with a wrong that has been done to you. When you hold on to the sins of others, it is difficult to see God's action in your life. Jesus urged forgiveness. Just as God let go of our sin because of Jesus' death for us, we are called to let go of the sins against us. God doesn't ask us to condone wrongdoing or hurt. He simply bids us to let Him take care of it. Forgiveness clears our souls of clutter and lets us be attentive to His gracious action in our lives.

How do you watch for God's responses? First, be attentive to God's Word. Psalm 119:130 says, "The unfolding of Your words gives light." When you're looking for the answers to your prayers, look in the Bible. Find a spot that might deal with what you're asking, or be attentive as you read a book of the Bible or some devotional material. Let God do the talking. Be quiet and let Him have His say.

Next, take some time. A pastor I know told me that his prayer time consists of 20 percent talking and 80 percent listening—just taking time to see what God will bring. I've learned that as I've faced major decisions. I need time to keep watch. I need to give God room to answer. I like the word *unfolding* in Psalm 119:130. Day-by-day, you can watch to see God's answers unfold. In my opinion, this is an exciting part of prayer. It's wonderful to watch and see how God will respond to prayer. When you make a commitment to watch, you become extra attentive to what's happening around you. You truly wait in expectation for God to respond.

Finally, talk. Take what you've seen in God's Word and what you've heard and noticed around you, and talk it over with a prayer partner, with your husband or wife, or with a Christian friend. When you talk with another believer, you gain perspective and accountability. You allow someone else to evaluate your conclusions according to God's Word. Sometimes, you receive clarity and encouragement when you're doubting what is, in reality, a very clear answer from God. Talk helps give you clarity. Psalm 91 says, "When he calls Me, I will answer him" (v. 15). God promises answers. We are called to watch.

How to Pray: Keep Going

One thing is certain: the devil doesn't want you to pray. Satan would much rather have you become burned out, exhausted, depressed, and disillusioned with God. He would love it if you said, "Prayer? I don't have time for it! I don't want to try it! It's awkward for me. I feel like I'm no good at it. I think I'll bypass prayer and try to tough it out myself."

Jesus knew this would happen. That's why He warned His disciples about this spiritual warfare when He taught them to pray, "And lead us not into temptation, but deliver us from evil" (Matthew 6:13). If God is working in your life, you can expect Satan to fight Him every step of the way. If you venture into prayer, you need to be aware that the devil will try to stop you. He doesn't want you to call upon God. He doesn't want you to see God's love and care for you as you communicate with Him. So Jesus gave prayer instruction that hits the enemy head-on. He let you know that God will fight for you every step of the way. The gift of prayer brings you to the cross and to the risen Lord. It is a gift that lets you say, "Jesus, my Savior, the one committed to my life, *do Your thing*! Battle away for me!" And battle He does. The ultimate Answer to your prayers is fighting for you. The living Lord Jesus Christ never lets up in His work to save and sustain you.

So keep going. You will get tired. You may feel awkward. Doubts will come. Words may not come easily. But God keeps fighting for you. In fact, the Bible says that the Holy Spirit prays for you when all you can do is groan (Romans 8:26). The Bible assures you that even Jesus intercedes for you as He reigns on high with the Father (v. 34). Keep going because your Savior keeps going too.

I'll never forget a wedding rehearsal I had a long time ago. As I was waiting for everyone to arrive, a member of the wedding party walked in. He said hello, saw that we weren't ready to start, and asked me, "Would you mind if I prayed?" I said, "Go right ahead."

He told me, "My pastor is a man of prayer. I want to be a man of prayer too." Then he walked to the front pew, knelt down, and prayed. When I saw this big guy devoted to prayer, I thought to myself, I want to be like that. I want to be a person of prayer. I want my church to be a church of prayer. And that is the course we charted as we delighted in God's precious gift of communication with Him.

YOUR ANSWER TO PRAYER

Human beings crave transcendence. We crave a connection beyond the ordinary here-and-now. To be given the gift of prayer—conversation with God—meets a deep and abiding yearning in our lives. But more than the gift of prayer, we are given the ultimate answer to our prayers. Each prayer we pray shows that we are not self-sufficient. We need God's listening ear. Whether we are asking for healing, peace, or provision; whether we are crying out in thanksgiving or praise; or whether we are confiding in God and asking Him our biggest questions, we express our own incompleteness and ongoing need for God's help. So, before we could even ask for it, God answered our greatest need by sending His only Son, our Savior Jesus Christ.

In Luke 2, the lowly shepherds watched their flocks in the wee hours of the night. These men were outcasts and lowlifes in the eyes of the "righteous" Jews. Stinky shepherds who violated religious laws were not the "in crowd" and were not respected by the religious elite. Imagine how they felt. You may understand what it feels like to be excluded and looked down upon. But it was to those shepherds that God decided to reveal the greatest news in all of history. Luke 2 recounts the announcement of the angel: "Fear not, for behold, I bring you good news of great joy that will be for all the people. For unto you is born this day in the city of David a Savior, who is Christ the Lord" (vv. 10–12).

Then a multitude of angels appeared to them saying, "Glory to God in the highest, and on earth peace, good will toward men" (v. 14 KJV). I like that King James Version translation because each segment of the angels' message directs us to the Answer to all our prayers. Finally, here on earth, the Glory of God has appeared as God promised long ago. Finally, the Peace of God in Jesus Christ had come among us. The Prince of Peace was born. Finally, the Good Will of God, His Favor in the flesh, made His home with us. God was not far away. He was with us. He was exactly what we needed. He is exactly what we crave. He is the answer to our prayers.

Notes

1. Paul McCain, ed., *Concordia: The Lutheran Confessions*, second edition (St. Louis: Concordia Publishing House, 2006), 410-11.

Study Guide for Chapter Four

Your Answer to Prayer

1. Read Philippians 4:6–7. What help does prayer provide and what promises come with a life of prayer?

2. Read 1 Timothy 2:1–6. How do these verses shape our prayers, teach us for whom to pray, and reinforce the proper motivation for prayer?

Jesus taught His disciples to pray by teaching them what we call "The Lord's Prayer." Martin Luther said:

> We should be moved and drawn to prayer. For in addition to this commandment and promise, God expects us and He Himself arranges the words and form of prayer for us. He places them on our lips for how and what we should pray [Psalm 51:15], so that we may see how heartily He pities us in our distress [Psalm 4:1], and we may never doubt that such prayer is pleasing to Him and shall certainly be answered. This <the Lord's Prayer> is a great advantage indeed over all other prayers that we might compose ourselves. For in our own prayers the conscience would ever be in doubt and say, "I have prayed, but who knows if it pleases Him or whether I have hit upon the right proportions and form?" Therefore, there is no nobler prayer to be found upon earth than the Lord's Prayer. We pray it daily [Matthew 6:11], because it has this excellent testimony, that God loves to hear it. We ought

not to surrender this for all the riches of the world.[1]

This is the Lord's Prayer in the Christian Church:

Our Father who art in heaven, hallowed be Thy name, Thy kingdom come, Thy will be done on earth as it is in heaven. Give us this day our daily bread; and forgive us our trespasses as we forgive those who trespass against us; and lead us not into temptation, but deliver us from evil. For Thine is the kingdom and the power and the glory forever and ever. Amen.

3. Look at each petition of the Lord's Prayer. Discuss what it means and how it relates to your life today.

4. Read Ephesians 6:18–20. The apostle Paul includes prayer at the end of his discussion about spiritual armor. How is prayer a "weapon" of faith and, according to these verses, what can prayer accomplish?

5. Read 1 Thessalonians 5:16–18. What does it mean to "pray without ceasing"?

6. Why is it important to know that part of God's will for us is that we pray?

7. Loneliness is a pervasive problem. How does the blessing of prayer fill a need we have as human beings?

8. Sometimes, God answers our prayers with a yes, sometimes He says no, and at other times, we need to wait. Share answers you've seen God give to some of your prayers and how those answers have shaped your life.

9. Talk about how Jesus is the ultimate answer to all prayer.

FIVE

YOUR HELP IN TROUBLE

GOD'S PRESENCE

Have you ever had to run for your life?

I sat with my friend Bo listening to his African guest describe his harrowing escape after tribal fury erupted in his home country. With just a few minutes' notice, he ran into the darkness from his home. Over his shoulder, fires erupted in his village as machete-wielding thugs searched for bloodshed to satisfy their ethnic-cleansing lust.

We sat together on a breezy South Texas day. Our shaded adobe-style patio and delicious brunch of fresh fruit, cold juice, and tasty bakery treats created a serene and lazy atmosphere. The beauty and comfort around us stood in stark contrast to the terror being described at the table.

Gasping for breath that night in Africa, our friend stumbled into a stand of thick brush. Well concealed from his adversaries, he looked back and forth in desperation. He thought his family had made it out, but they were nowhere in sight. He had felt sure that his parents and two sisters were right behind him, but something must have happened. Hesitating only to say a prayer, he bolted out of the brush and sprinted back toward the danger.

The smoke and fire blinded him. He heard shrieks of pain coming from every home and every street. Darting through the shadows, he entered his family's compound. The house was ablaze, and the criminals were gone. He glanced at a small shed in the back corner of the property and ran to the open door. That's when he heard a whimper coming from the darkness inside. In a whisper, he called his father's name. A hand reached out and grabbed his arm—causing him to pull away and sending his pulse skyrocketing. But then he saw a miraculous sight. It was his father! Somehow, they had been spared. Somehow, his family was safe. At that moment, he knew they were not alone.

Hiding in the shadows, the family crept out of the compound and rushed into the jungle on the outskirts of the village. Our African friend described the remarkable sense of peace and confidence as the whole family escaped the melee of violence. With constant prayer on their hearts and from their lips, they made it to safety.

"God was present," the African guest told us as we sat transfixed at the table. "I have no doubt that the only way we made it out alive was by the protecting hand of almighty God. He was with us. I know He was with us."

THE LIFE WE CRAVE

I listened to our friend's story with awe, but I also listened with some envy. I didn't have any desire to be in the life-threatening situation he and his family experienced, but his sense of God's presence awakened a deep craving of my soul. The mundane and sometimes tedious routines of this life grow old and tiring. But to see and sense the work of God—how could anything be better?

I know I'm not alone. In his book *Windows of the Soul*, Ken Gire quotes Garrison Keillor: "If you can't go to church and at least for a moment be given transcendence, if you can't pass briefly from this life into the next, then I can't see why anyone should go. Just a brief moment of transcendence causes you to come out of church a changed person."[1]

People are looking for more than this life gives. People crave transcendence, something beyond what we ordinarily experience and perceive, something bigger than ourselves, something with greater meaning and significance. People crave the presence and work of God.

No matter how popular or unpopular organized religion or church might be, human beings know there's more to this life than eating, sleeping, working, paying bills, taking care of the yard, watching the news, and enduring the day-to-day grind. The Bible says that God "has put eternity into man's heart" (Ecclesiastes 3:11). More than that, God shouts the fact of His existence and presence to us over and over again:

> The heavens declare the glory of God, and the sky
> above proclaims His handiwork. Day to day pours out
> speech, and night to night reveals knowledge. There
> is no speech, nor are there words, whose voice is not
> heard. Their voice goes out through all the earth, and
> their words to the end of the world. (Psalm 19:1–4)

But God is even more specific about His presence than setting eternity in our hearts and pouring forth His speech from creation. He appeared personally to us in Jesus. The apostle John wrote, "The Word became flesh and dwelt among us, and we have seen His glory, glory as of the only Son from the Father, full of grace and truth" (John 1:14).

God showed up. The transcendent God of the universe became present among us! Crowds followed Him. People were amazed and transformed by His miracles. The world was shocked and awed by His death on a cross and His resurrection from the grave on the first Easter Sunday. Jesus was and still is a mystery unmatched in the history of the world. He is even called "the mystery of God" (Colossians 2:2 NIV).

More than that, we still mingle with the mystery of God's presence. When Jesus broke bread and poured wine at His last Passover meal, He instituted a meal of His mysterious and miraculous presence for the forgiveness of our sins. The apostle Paul even declared about himself and his fellow servants, "This is how one should regard us, as servants of Christ and stewards of the mysteries of God" (1 Corinthians 4:1).

Jesus even promised, "I am with you always, to the end of the age" (Matthew 28:20). This was not a metaphorical expression of an imagined spiritual experience. Jesus was not using a figure of speech. He promised to be with us. For us, as sin-broken people on the run from the crushing tests and trials of life, this was the foundational purpose of our Savior. The Gospel of Matthew tells us about the birth of Jesus: "All this took place to fulfill what the Lord had spoken by the prophet: 'Behold, the virgin shall conceive and bear a son, and they shall call His name Immanuel' (which means, God with us)" (Matthew 1:22–23). God is with us. We need Him to be with us, and He draws close. Now, because of Him, there *is* more to this life. He is present. No moment is ordinary. No task is mundane. No person is run-of-the-mill. By God's grace, each moment is a transcendent moment. Each day is filled with mystery. The life God gives is the life we crave.

REMOVING THE WELCOME MAT

But how could we ever be worthy of such a gift? How could we welcome God into our humble and flawed lives? After all, we're not people a Holy God would want to hang around. Romans 3 is brutally honest about it:

> As it is written: "None is righteous, no, not one; no one understands; no one seeks for God. All have turned aside; together they have become worthless; no one does good, not even one." "Their throat is an open grave; they use their tongues to deceive." "The venom of asps is under their lips." "Their mouth is full of curses and bitterness." "Their feet are swift to shed blood; in their paths are ruin and misery, and the way of peace they have not known." "There is no fear of God before their eyes." (vv. 10–18)

The apostle Paul quotes several psalms in this section of Scripture. He makes the case for what we can see clearly when we look in the mirror: we're sinful, rebellious people who would rather take control of our own lives than let God have any say about who we are and what we do. It's sad, but it's the truth. We would rather turn away from God than welcome Him into our lives. We resemble the king who took over for Nebuchadnezzar, a man named Belshazzar.

Belshazzar was a descendant of Nebuchadnezzar—his son or perhaps his grandson. The only episode we know about his life is the one we hear about in Daniel 5. The young Belshazzar was a party kind of guy. Like some heirs to wealth and position, this new king enjoyed the perks of power more than he participated in the work toward power. Belshazzar thought it would be a good idea to use the gold and silver cups Nebuchadnezzar had taken from the temple of the Lord in Jerusalem for party dinnerware. He invited thousands of his "best friends" to drink wine from these vessels as they worshiped "the gods of gold and silver, bronze, iron, wood, and stone" (Daniel 5:4). With gusto, wives, concubines, friends, and advisers engaged in the pagan revelry. They spurned and mocked the Most High God.

It was not a pretty picture.

You may be reading this and thinking, What an awful situation! How could anyone ever do that? Or you may be scanning this text and thinking to yourself, This sounds like the people I hang around! The bottom line is this: we're never far from chaos, grief, strife, and every variety of dysfunction in our own lives. We start to accumulate the baggage of trouble and rebellion from the very beginning. Psalm 51 says, "Surely I was sinful at birth, sinful from the time my mother conceived me" (v. 5 NIV).

Any one of us can make life miserable. We hurt ourselves. We are cranky and hurtful toward others. We disobey God and stray from His ways. My wife tells the story of the time her mother stopped the car, told her and her brother to get out, and drove away. Her mother was fed up with their bickering. She couldn't take it anymore. It had to stop. So she ordered them to get out of the car, and off she went. And she didn't just go around the block to prove a point. She didn't come back, apologize for losing her cool, and make amends by taking them for ice cream on the way home. No, she drove home and stayed there. My wife and her brother walked down a hill to where their father worked and waited for their dad to drive them home. Trying to explain the events that led to their stranding didn't endear them to their father. A lesson was learned that day. Of course, that was in a different day and age, a different era of parenting. But even though discipline methods have changed, you can probably understand that kind of exasperation. You know what it feels like to reach your limit. There may have been times you've walked away. What's puzzling and amazing, however, is that God doesn't "throw us out of the car," even though we deserve it. Even when all-out rebellion is happening, God still pursues us.

That's what He did for Daniel. Twenty-two years had passed since King Nebuchadnezzar's death. A new era had been ushered in. Belshazzar's party was indicative of that new season. The Most High God was opposed, and the exiles from Jerusalem were scorned. At best, the foreigners from Judah were cast aside as people who didn't belong. At worst, they may have been persecuted and imprisoned. Where was Daniel during this time? We don't know. But we do know he was forgotten. He was a despised outsider during dark decades of oppressive Babylonian rule.

Then God stepped in. Daniel tells us that during Belshazzar's party, fingers of a human hand appeared and wrote on the plaster of the king's palace. It was wake-up time for Belshazzar. We are told that "the king's color changed, and his thoughts alarmed him; his limbs gave way, and his knees knocked together" (Daniel 5:6). This man was scared. And behind the knocking knees of Belshazzar was God's pursuit of His servant Daniel. By this time, Daniel was an older man. He had been captured as a teenager, had spent over forty years serving Nebuchadnezzar, had been cast aside by Belshazzar for over two decades, and now probably wondered what his fate might ultimately be. Were his years of testifying for the Lord a waste of time? Would history remember him as a has-been, someone who tried to stand up for the Most High God but saw the effort fizzle out? No, God wouldn't stand for that. Trouble would not have the last word.

A frightened Belshazzar called for his advisers and wise men. Surely someone could understand what the writing on the wall said. The king promised, "Whoever reads this writing, and shows me its interpretation, shall be clothed with purple and have a chain of gold around his neck and shall be the third ruler in the kingdom" (v. 7). But it was "like déjà vu all over again." No one could read the writing. The wise men were perplexed. And the king became more frightened than ever.

That's when the queen spoke up. We don't know if this was Belshazzar's mother or grandmother (sometimes the word *father* is used as a word for "descendant"), but whoever it was, she remembered Daniel. She told Belshazzar:

> There is a man in your kingdom in whom is the spirit
> of the holy gods. In the days of your father, light and
> understanding and wisdom like the wisdom of the
> gods were found in him, and King Nebuchadnezzar,
> your father—your father the king—made him chief
> of the magicians, enchanters, Chaldeans, and astrolo-
> gers, because an excellent spirit, knowledge, and un-
> derstanding to interpret dreams, explain riddles, and
> solve problems were found in this Daniel, whom the
> king named Belteshazzar. Now let Daniel be called,
> and he will show the interpretation. (vv. 11–12)

The voice of an advocate brought Daniel out of obscurity. God was making sure the message of life in Him prevailed. And Daniel, after so many years, was still receiving help in his trouble.

Trouble does not disappear with age. Burdens do not limit themselves to the young and brash. Worries do not fade as the wisdom of age increases. In fact, the opposite is sometimes true. When I was younger and churches interviewed me for potential positions, one topic invariably came up: "Talk about some of your greatest failures and how you handled them." Every time I heard the question, I strained to think of my failures. After all, I was a faithful worker. I tried my best. I did a pretty good job. What failures could I mention? In those early days, I was stumped. But now, things have changed. My failures? I've got big lists. I have lists for my professional life, my personal life, and my family life. I could fill hours talking about my failures. I've been disheartened by my failures, embarrassed by my fumbling, and humiliated by my faux pas. These days, I understand that while young people do mess up, it takes a little bit of time to see real failure. If you have trouble spotting your foibles and faults, take some time to live. Let the years go by. Take a stab at challenges like marriage and parenting. Live a few decades in the ups and downs of a career. Experience life's temptations and trials for a good chunk of a century. That's when failures show up in a big way.

I'll never forget ministering to a few older men when they were close to death. Some of them were tormented by their burdens and failures in life. Good men, godly men, were harassed by regrets and wrongdoing. The devil was trying to create doubt and despair in their hearts and minds. These men needed to hear the true and consoling call of Christ: "Come to Me, all who labor and are heavy laden, and I will give you rest. Take My yoke upon you, and learn from Me, for I am gentle and lowly in heart, and you will find rest for your souls. For My yoke is easy, and My burden is light" (Matthew 11:28–30). They needed what we all need: real help in times of trouble.

Daniel needed help in trouble too. And God provided it during a time of wilderness and pain. So Daniel was brought before the king, who started the conversation with a condescending tone: "You are that Daniel, one of the exiles of Judah, whom the king my father brought from Judah" (Daniel 5:13). Daniel was put in his place by the petrified king. Then the king went on to ask for help, promising a great reward if Daniel solved this puzzle. But Daniel replied, "Let your gifts be for yourself, and give your rewards to another. Nevertheless, I will read the writing to the king and make known to him the interpretation" (v. 17).

Daniel didn't hold back when it came to bringing God's bold and honest message to the corrupt king. Daniel reviewed history with Belshazzar. He told the king about Nebuchadnezzar's debacle of arrogance, his seven-year stint of insanity. He told the king about Nebuchadnezzar's humility, his repentant heart that acknowledged God as the ruler of all things. But then he said to Belshazzar:

> And you his son, Belshazzar, have not humbled your heart, though you knew all this, but you have lifted up yourself against the Lord of heaven. And the vessels of His house have been brought in before you, and you and your lords, your wives, and your concubines have drunk wine from them. And you have praised the gods of silver and gold, of bronze, iron, wood, and stone, which do not see or hear or know, but the God in whose hand is your breath, and whose are all your ways, you have not honored.

Then from His presence the hand was sent, and this writing was inscribed. And this is the writing that was inscribed: MENE, MENE, TEKEL, and PARSIN. This is the interpretation of the matter: MENE, God has numbered the days of your kingdom and brought it to an end; TEKEL, you have been weighed in the balances and found wanting; PERES, your kingdom is divided and given to the Medes and Persians. (vv. 22–28)

Daniel spoke with painful honesty. Refreshing, isn't it? The smooth fakery and flattery of the world can feel good for a while. The promises of happiness from the latest products may give us a temporary high. Living in the illusion of eating, drinking, and being merry may last for a time. But at some point, we crave honesty. We crave reality. We yearn for truth. And God doesn't disappoint us. Karl Marx said that religion is the opiate of the people—a soothing anesthetic to life's realities that allows people to live in a numbed dream world. Marx clearly did not understand the Bible's message or Christianity's foundations. It is anything but an opiate. God opens up with total candor about our sinful and hopeless condition. He does not hold back. His Word unleashes painful honesty—as we saw previously in Romans 3, in Psalm 51, and in Daniel's honest message to Belshazzar. God cares enough to let us know where we really stand. Finally. Someone who levels with us. Then, as our knees are knocking and our faces grow pale in terror and repentance, God speaks another honest word. It is a word of rescue and help in our deep and dire trouble: Jesus came to bear the burden of our sin and to take the full consequences of our failures. He came to save us.

Psalm 46:1–3 says, "God is our refuge and strength, a very

present help in trouble. Therefore we will not fear though the earth gives way, though the mountains be moved into the heart of the sea, though its waters roar and foam, though the mountains tremble at its swelling." Daniel discovered that in a powerful way. After waiting for decades, God stepped in to help. The unrepentant and prideful Belshazzar paid the price for his arrogant wrongdoing: "That very night Belshazzar the Chaldean king was killed. And Darius the Mede received the kingdom, being about sixty-two years old" (Daniel 5:30–31). The Babylonian kingdom saw its end. The Medo-Persian Empire now took over. But the Most High God was still working to make His grace and truth known. He continued to walk with Daniel. And when more trouble developed under King Darius, God would once again prove to be Daniel's refuge, strength, and salvation.

COMING CLEAN

What was the difference between Daniel and Belshazzar? Why was a wealthy and powerful king so miserable and a captive exile so confident? Why did God's presence make Belshazzar a nervous wreck while it transformed Daniel from a forgotten prisoner into a bold prophet? Could it be that utter honesty before God causes changes that run deep into the heart and soul?

The craving for God's help in the face of burdensome trouble has been seen for decades as millions of people have sought freedom from addiction by using a twelve-step program. Alcoholics Anonymous originated the Twelve Steps in the 1930s.[2] It's amazing how an answer to alcoholism and other addictions has been found in simple transparency and honesty before God and others. More than half of the Twelve Steps deal with coming clean. They emphasize complete confession:

Step 1:   We admitted we were powerless over alcohol—that
            our lives had become unmanageable.

Step 4:   Made a searching and fearless moral inventory of
            ourselves.

Step 5:   Admitted to God, to ourselves, and to another hu-
            man being the exact nature of our wrongs.

Step 6:   Were entirely ready to have God remove all these
            defects of character.

Step 7:   Humbly asked Him to remove our shortcomings.

Step 8:   Made a list of all the persons we had harmed, and
            became willing to make amends to them all.

Step 10:   Continued to take personal inventory and when we
            were wrong, promptly admitted it.[3]

As the saying goes, "Confession is good for the soul." Programs like AA understand that. They understand the potent impact of confession. It's one powerful way God gives us help in trouble. God graciously allows us to lay our burdens down, to be freed from the guilt, pain, and trouble that pile on our shoulders. Instead of relegating us to live in denial about the heavy weight of our failures, shortcomings, sin, and flaws, God levels with us and gives us a gracious remedy. The apostle John said, "If we say we have no sin, we deceive ourselves, and the truth is not in us. If we confess our sins, He is faithful and just to forgive us our sins and to cleanse us from all unrighteousness" (1 John 1:8–9).

When I was in college and seminary, I carried a backpack full of books to my classes. The books were heavy. The load was not light. When I walked uphill, I remember having to bend forward to balance my academic cargo. If I didn't, I would fall backward down the incline. Occasionally, a friend would walk up behind me and pick up the backpack while it was on my back. Suddenly, I was burden free! I felt light and able to stand up straight. It was liberating—until my friend let go of the load abruptly and let it fall heavily, bending me backward. He laughed, but I groaned. Once again, I was in bondage to my books.

The baggage we accumulate in life becomes too heavy to carry around. Like a backpack filled with heavy books, wounds from childhood, regrets in relationships, personal failures, and bad decisions pile up and weigh us down. But God has provided a solution. He takes the burdens. He lifts the backpack off our shoulders. He gives us the Good News that Jesus took every foul-up, every disappointment, every shortcoming, and every sin that would have created an unmanageable load and an unrepayable debt in our lives. The Bible addresses this debt and burden of sin: "This [God] set aside, nailing it to the cross" (Colossians 2:14).

What better gift could there be than a fresh start, a new beginning because of God's forgiveness? The Bible says, "Therefore, if anyone is in Christ, he is a new creation. The old has passed away; behold, the new has come" (2 Corinthians 5:17).

Martin Luther commented on the gift of confessing sins. He said, "For the Christian way essentially consists in acknowledging ourselves to be sinners and in praying for grace."[4] The craving to be released from our burdens is so powerful, Luther noted, that people's "own conscience would so drive and disturb him that he would be glad to do what a poor and miserable beggar does when he hears that a rich gift of money or clothing is being handed out at a certain place. So as not to miss it, he would run there as fast as he can and would need no bailiff to beat and drive him on."[5] Luther then encouraged, "If you are poor and miserable, then go to

Confession and make use of its healing medicine. He who feels his misery and need will no doubt develop such a longing for it that he will run toward it with joy."[6]

The life we crave is a life that receives help in trouble, relief from our burdens, and rescue from what takes life out of us. Author, teacher, and priest Henri Nouwen described how burdens accumulate and how those encumbering weights pull us away from God:

> After twenty years in the academic world as a teacher of pastoral psychology, pastoral theology, and Christian spirituality, I began to experience a deep inner threat. As I entered into my fifties and was able to realize the unlikelihood of doubling my years, I came face to face with the simple question, "Did becoming older bring me closer to Jesus?" After twenty-five years of priesthood, I found myself praying poorly, living somewhat isolated from other people, and very much preoccupied with burning issues. Everyone was saying that I was doing really well, but something inside was telling me that my success was putting my own soul in danger. I began to ask myself whether my lack of contemplative prayer, my loneliness, and my constantly changing involvement in what seemed most urgent were signs that the Spirit was gradually being suppressed. It was very hard for me to see clearly, and though I never spoke about hell or only jokingly so, I woke up one day with the realization that I was living in a very dark place and that the term "burnout" was a convenient psychological translation for a spiritual death.[7]

Henri Nouwen started to come clean. He began a journey of letting God peel away the veneer of his life, the pretense, the denial, the busyness, the pride, and the failure. Nouwen began to experience freedom as Jesus took the burdens from him and led him to a renewed life of service, simplicity, and self-sacrifice.

King David understood the power of confession and forgiveness. He said, "Blessed is the one whose transgression is forgiven, whose sin is covered" (Psalm 32:1). David knew what it was like to carry the load of backbreaking failure and regret. He wooed another man's wife into an adulterous relationship. He lied to the woman's husband and, ultimately, orchestrated his murder. He brought the widow into his palace and made her his wife in order to try to save face and look heroic. But inside, as Henri Nouwen said, his soul was in danger. Keeping his weakness and transgression to himself eroded his very being. David declared, "For when I kept silent, my bones wasted away through my groaning all day long. For day and night Your hand was heavy upon me; my strength was dried up as by the heat of summer" (vv. 3–4). No one can carry the load life piles on. It's only a matter of time before you become weighed down with groaning, sadness, bitterness, disappointment, or weariness. So David spoke of the remedy. He lauded the grace of God, the gift of being able to cast all his cares on his Savior:

> I acknowledged my sin to You, and I did not cover my iniquity; I said, "I will confess my transgressions to the LORD," and You forgave the iniquity of my sin. Therefore let everyone who is godly offer prayer to You at a time when You may be found; surely in the rush of great waters, they shall not reach him. You are

a hiding place for me; You preserve me from trouble;
You surround me with shouts of deliverance. (vv. 5–7)

Do you need to lay your burdens at the feet of the One who gives you help in trouble? Jesus said, "Come to Me, all who labor and are heavy laden, and I will give you rest" (Matthew 11:28). The life you crave is life under the grace of God. It is not a life of denial, suppression, or running away. It is not a life of drowning your sorrows or displacing your anger or punishing yourself. It is life that has the burden removed, the pain relieved, and the pressure soothed. The price wasn't cheap. Confession of sin is not a "get out of jail free" card that you flip back onto the game board as you go your merry way. The cost for the removal of our sin was the life of the Son of God. His brutal death and abandonment by God is the result of casting our cares upon Him. The gift is grace with great gravity. It's serious business that moves our hearts and causes us to fall down in worship and thanksgiving. At the cost of His Son, God is our help in trouble.

LIVING IN CONFESSION AND FORGIVENESS

The Bible tells us how radical and redeeming God's forgiveness is. As far as the east is from the west, He removes sin and guilt from our lives (Psalm 103:12). Though our sins are like scarlet, He makes them white as snow (Isaiah 1:18). Even though we were dead in our sins and transgressions, God has made us alive with Jesus Christ—not because we earned or deserved such restoration, but because of His grace and love for us (Ephesians 2:1–5).

We confess. God absolves. God lets go. God moved every ounce of sin from our lives and placed it all on Jesus, His Son, as

He died a torturous death and was cast away from God's presence on the cross. Jesus paid the penalty, the high price for our dark and sin-stained souls. Jesus removed the junk from our lives—freely and graciously. We no longer live in the accumulation of sin's garbage—in dumps littered with the stench of our own imperfection. Jesus took that garbage out and continues to put it on the curb as His Word washes us clean, as Baptism cleanses us, and as the Lord's Supper renews our souls.

God's saving work reminds me of the personal dumpster I have at home. Actually, I have two. The city gave each homeowner a set of gargantuan dumpsters for trash and recycling. Each one is on wheels. These massive bins replaced reasonably sized garbage cans and recycling containers. Now, the thunderous roll of dumpsters is heard echoing throughout our neighborhood twice each week. Once the dumpsters have been set at the curb, an automatic garbage collection truck screeches to a halt outside each home, lowers a clawlike mechanism, snatches the dumpster from its place, dumps the debris hastily into the truck, and returns the monstrous container akimbo to the street-side spot (sometimes it's akimbo; I just wanted to use that word). We neighborhood dwellers then obediently roll our empty personal dumpsters back to their nesting places. The containers are so large, I have to open the main garage door to put mine back—as if I'm driving a vehicle into the garage. The dumpster doesn't fit through the little side door. But more power to it! My personal dumpster holds a lot of garbage. And that's exactly what I need. I can load it up with some pretty nasty stuff. It all fits inside. When Tuesday comes, it's all gone. Time for a new beginning.

God gives each of us a "personal dumpster." Ephesians 4:31–32 says, "Get rid of all bitterness, rage and anger, brawling and slander, along with every form of malice. Be kind and compassionate to one another, forgiving each other, just as in Christ God forgave you" (NIV). That is an invitation to some serious dumpster action. As we get rid of our junk, confessing to our Savior, He carts it away through His action for you—living, suffering, bleeding, dying, and rising. Each day and every moment, through Word and Sacrament, you have an empty dumpster, a new beginning, a lightened life. You can even take some of the trash from others and empty their dumpsters by forgiving them "as in Christ God forgave you." The Bible says, "Therefore, confess your sins to one another and pray for one another, that you may be healed" (James 5:16).

What a precious gift we've been given! We've received help in trouble. God has spoken the honest truth to us. He's confronted us with our sin. He's shown us our garbage—the stink and all. Then He calls us to bring it all to Him, to place the foul-smelling and life-poisoning burden on Him.

This is what each of us needs so desperately. And it is what the world yearns to hear. Belshazzar would have been bothered by the thunderous roll of personal dumpsters. But, by God's grace, the sound is music to our ears. Let's let the thunderous roll be heard—as God makes the world and our lives a cleaner place with His grace. In trouble, it's the help we crave.

Notes

1. Ken Gire, *Windows of the Soul* (Grand Rapids: Zonder van, 1996), 120.

2. www.aa.org/aatimeline/

3. www.aa.org/en_pdfs/smf-121_en.pdf

4. Paul McCain, ed., *Concordia: The Lutheran Confessions*, second edition (St. Louis: Concordia Publishing House, 2006), 650.

5. McCain, 652.

6. McCain, 652.

7. Henri Nouwen, *In the Name of Jesus* (New York: Cross-road, 1994), 10–11.

STUDY GUIDE FOR CHAPTER FIVE

YOUR HELP IN TROUBLE

1. Read Joshua 1:5–9. How have you seen God present with you in your walk of faith? Share some key moments or events when you have been certain of His presence.

2. King Belshazzar didn't listen to the proclamations of his predecessor, Nebuchadnezzar. In fact, the new king seemed to follow a completely opposite path. How does a spirit of rebellion and orneriness show itself in your life and in the sinful behavior you slide into?

3. Daniel didn't pull any punches with Belshazzar, and God doesn't pull any punches with us when it comes to our faults and failures. How is God's honesty both difficult and refreshing in contrast to what our culture offers us?

4. Read James 5:16–19. These verses take place in the context of the community of believers helping one another. Talk about what is risky, frightening, and healthy in living a life of confession before God and fellow believers.

5. Read Psalm 51:1–13. The heading for the psalm reads, "To the choirmaster. A Psalm of David, when Nathan the prophet went to him, after he had gone in to Bathsheba." If you're not familiar with the account of David and Bathsheba, read 2 Samuel 11. Knowing what David did, what surprises you about his requests in Psalm 51?

6. What do David's words tell you about God's character, David's understanding of God, and the result of God's forgiveness?

7. To forgive means "to let go." Read Romans 6:6–11, 22–23. How did God let go of your sins?

8. Read Matthew 18:21–22. Jesus indicates that forgiveness requires persistently letting go of wrongs. What does it mean to practice ongoing forgiveness with yourself and with others?

9. Read Daniel 9:4–19. This is a beautiful prayer of confession by Daniel. What qualities of true confession stand out to you from Daniel's prayer? Talk about how you might integrate these into your life.

SIX

"But when the goodness and loving kindness of God our Savior appeared, He saved us, not because of works done by us in righteousness, but according to His own mercy, by the washing of regeneration and renewal of the Holy Spirit." Titus 3:4–5

YOUR NEW BEGINNING

CRAVING A DEEPER CONNECTION

Timothy Treadwell wanted to do something meaningful with his life. He tried school. He tried acting. But nothing captured his imagination. He drifted into life on the party circuit, becoming addicted to alcohol and drugs. Then a defining moment happened. He overdosed on illegal drugs. Hitting rock bottom and nearly losing his life, he knew something had to change. That's when a friend helped him through his addiction problems and suggested that he travel to Alaska to watch bears. So Timothy went.

Bears became Timothy's passion. He began to spend summers at the Katmai National Park and Preserve in Alaska. He established a nonprofit organization to help protect and build appreciation for bears. But he also took risks. Timothy began to believe he had a special connection with the Katmai grizzly bears. He gave them names and videotaped his interactions with them, at times crawling on all fours while singing softly and approaching the bears to touch them. He ignored National Park Service guidelines, not carrying bear spray to defend himself and not relocating his camp according to the Park Service safety rules. Appearing on *Late Show with David Letterman* in 2001, Treadwell described Alaska brown bears as mostly harmless "party animals."

Treadwell reveled in his relationship with wild animals. He said his personal bond with the bears inspired him to give up drugs. He found the deeper connection and purpose he craved.

But in the fall of 2003, disaster struck. While camping in an area he called "the bear maze," a heavily traveled intersection of bear trails, Treadwell and his girlfriend were confronted by an aggressive and hungry bear. Both Treadwell and his girlfriend were killed. In spite of the many warnings from Park Service officials and biologists, Treadwell had insisted on pursuing personal and close contact with dangerous creatures. His desire for a connection with something more than what the conventional world offered led to personal discoveries and many thrills, but ultimately it led to tragedy.[1]

Timothy Treadwell is not the only person who pursued something deeper and more fulfilling in life. The yearning for a connection beyond what the ordinary world offers has motivated daring explorations, new scientific discoveries, and provocative theories about life and existence. This search for meaning has ruined many lives as well. From life-risking adventures to experimentation with the excesses of life to the accumulation of pleasure-promising material things, many people have fallen into misery and destruction as they try to discover a sense of ultimate fulfillment.

I heard about the development of a 110-inch flat-screen television—the largest ever produced. Its price is $150,000! Can you imagine a Super Bowl party with that TV? I'm sure some people are lining up to buy this new high-resolution digital wonder. But by the time you're reading this book, I'm also sure that the biggest

TV is no longer the biggest—and the people who purchased it are wondering how to get their next big-screen thrill.

The truth is that the deeper connection we crave cannot be found in what we cause, discover, or produce. At best, seeking fulfillment in our own sphere of command and control will end in disappointment. At worst, this quest will end in our own destruction. Wise King Solomon said, "For with much wisdom comes much sorrow; the more knowledge, the more grief" (Ecclesiastes 1:18 NIV). Solomon tried everything. He indulged in pleasure and laughter. He drank fine wine and hobnobbed with beautiful women. He built great projects and listened to fine music. He accumulated riches and developed a portfolio that exceeded anything seen in history. He conquered kingdoms and surpassed the achievements of anyone who had ever occupied his position. He continued to be wise and discerning, every step of the way. But after seeking a "wow factor" in all the things of the world, Solomon summed up his search in this way:

> I denied myself nothing my eyes desired; I refused my heart no pleasure. My heart took delight in all my labor, and this was the reward for all my toil. Yet when I surveyed all that my hands had done and what I had toiled to achieve, everything was meaningless, a chasing after the wind. (Ecclesiastes 2:10–11 NIV)

WHERE THE REAL CONNECTION IS FOUND

Where can the deeper, more meaningful life be found? Daniel knew the answer. After King Darius took over, Daniel found himself alienated by the king's leadership team. Darius appointed a new staff of rulers, 120 men to oversee the kingdom. While Daniel was one of the three administrators who supervised this group, he was viewed by his colleagues as a foreign interloper. And when Daniel showed skill and aptitude greater than that of the other rulers, trouble began to brew:

> Then this Daniel became distinguished above all the other high officials and satraps, because an excellent spirit was in him. And the king planned to set him over the whole kingdom. Then the high officials and the satraps sought to find a ground for complaint against Daniel with regard to the kingdom. (Daniel 6:3–4)

But they couldn't find a thing wrong with Daniel. He wasn't corrupt. He did everything the king asked of him. He was never irresponsible. So the jealous officials decided to trap Daniel in what they viewed as his weakness: his faith. They said, "We shall not find any ground for complaint against this Daniel unless we find it in connection with the law of his God" (v. 5). So the plot began.

The devious high officials of the kingdom approached King Darius and told him that all the administrators, governors, prefects, and advisers agreed that the king should issue an edict that anyone who prayed to a god or man other than the king in the next thirty days should be thrown into the lions' den. This conniving caucus urged the king to put this proclamation into writing with his signature affixed to it so it could not be revoked—as was true of the laws of the Medes and Persians. Liking the idea, King Darius did as was suggested. He signed on the dotted line and rejoiced in the great loyalty of his trusted advisers.

Little did he know that Daniel had been left out of the loop. What did Daniel do when the pressure was on, when the peril was great, and when evil threatened him? What did he do when the world brought disappointment? He went back to his deep connection that transcended earthly life and temporal circumstances:

> When Daniel knew that the document had been signed, he went to his house where he had windows in his upper chamber open toward Jerusalem. He got down on his knees three times a day and prayed and gave thanks before his God, as he had done previously. (v. 10)

Daniel knew that a yearning for a connection beyond the ordinary world and a search for meaning and fulfillment in life were not satisfied by earthly pursuits, power, or pleasure. The deeper connection and ultimate fulfillment could be found only in God, who reaches into our lives from the outside and brings peace and satisfaction not offered by this world. Jesus said, "Peace I leave with you; My peace I give to you. Not as the world gives do I give to you. Let not your hearts be troubled, neither let them be afraid" (John 14:27). Only from the outside, from God reaching in, can a truly deep and ultimate connection be made in our lives. Only then can we experience genuine meaning that transcends what humanity can offer or conjure up.

So Daniel prayed—as he always did. And he got into big trouble. The tattletale officials found Daniel asking God for help. Immediately, they went to King Darius and reported the "crime." At this point in the narrative, we get a sense of how much Daniel had impressed and influenced the king: "Then the king, when he heard these words, was much distressed and set his mind to deliver Daniel. And he labored till the sun went down to rescue him" (Daniel 6:14). But in spite of his efforts, Darius could not find a way around this new law. Finally, he relented: "Then the king commanded, and Daniel was brought and cast into the den of lions. The king declared to Daniel, 'May your God, whom you serve continually, deliver you!'" (v. 16).

In addition to caring about Daniel, Darius knew about Daniel's faith and Daniel's God. Whether it was through direct conversation, the outward observation of Daniel's life, or both, Darius realized that something was different about this man. But whether Daniel's God could really come through, Darius didn't know. After the stone was placed over the opening of the lions' den, Darius couldn't eat or sleep all night.

The next morning, the dignified King Darius, ruler of the Medo-Persian Empire, ran to the den of lions and cried out, "O Daniel, servant of the living God, has your God, whom you serve continually, been able to deliver you from the lions?" (v. 20).

A voice came from the lion-infested lair: "O king, live forever! My God sent His angel and shut the lions' mouths, and they have not harmed me, because I was found blameless before Him; and also before you, O king, I have done no harm" (vv. 21–22). Daniel was alive! With great joy, the king ordered his men to lift Daniel from the den to begin his new life.

It really *was* a new life. Daniel had escaped certain death. There is a resurrection quality to this account. Like Jesus' tomb, a stone was rolled over the opening. Like that first Easter morning, an eager person raced to the place of death at dawn. And like the resurrected Jesus, the man who was thought never to be able to escape certain death was alive. This was a new and miraculous beginning for Daniel. And it was a new and miraculous beginning for everyone in King Darius's empire. Remember, this section of the Book of Daniel was written in Aramaic, the language of the world. Everybody in the kingdom and beyond would hear of this miracle. More than that, everyone would hear the truth that the key to a deep and meaningful life comes from the true God. The second half of Daniel 6:23 could serve as a five-star rating on the "Daniel.com" website: "So Daniel was taken up out of the den, and no kind of harm was found on him, because he had trusted in his God." *He had trusted in his God.* That's where new life comes from. That's how the miraculous happens. God reaches in. The true God intervenes. The Most High God shows up. The God of heaven protects.

And just in case anyone thought this was a fluke—a case of nauseous lions or a lions' den with a safe little corner—the next verse underscores the gravity of the lion-filled enclosure:

> And the king commanded, and those men who had maliciously accused Daniel were brought and cast into the den of lions—they, their children, and their wives. And before they reached the bottom of the den, the lions overpowered them and broke all their bones in pieces. (v. 24)

Miracle noted. Then we hear how the king issued another one of those declarations in the Book of Daniel that rattled the world's pursuit of meaning through ordinary, earthly diversions:

> Then King Darius wrote to all the peoples, nations, and languages that dwell in all the earth: "Peace be multiplied to you. I make a decree, that in all my royal

dominion people are to tremble and fear before the God of Daniel, for He is the living God, enduring forever; His kingdom shall never be destroyed, and His dominion shall be to the end. He delivers and rescues; He works signs and wonders in heaven and on earth, He who has saved Daniel from the power of the lions." (vv. 25–27)

The deep connection we're searching for has come down to meet us and help us. Will we open our eyes?

What about Today?

But does God really reach into our lives today?

Many would answer with an immediate and emphatic yes. Miracles happen today. Prayers are answered. Angel stories abound. God's help and wisdom are cited time and time again. But doubters and cynics have their say as well. They characterize miraculous events as figments of imagination or the results of wishful thinking.

But what if God reached into our lives in a way that was certain, verifiable, and even somewhat ordinary? What if God established points of contact that brought the deeper connection we crave into our lives in an accessible and simple way?

Fast-forward nearly six hundred years, and that is exactly what we see. Philip, a deacon appointed by the twelve disciples, was directed to travel to a desert road outside of Jerusalem. As he traveled the road, he encountered a man from Ethiopia, an official of Candace, the queen of the nation. The man was on his way home from Jerusalem, where he had spent time worshiping. As he traveled in his chariot, he read the Old Testament Book of Isaiah. Philip drew near, heard the man reading, and asked if he understood the text. The man replied, "How can I, unless someone guides me?" (Acts 8:31). Philip was then invited to sit in the chariot with him. He was reading verses from Isaiah 53:

> Like a sheep He was led to the slaughter and like a lamb before its shearer is silent, so He opens not His mouth. In His humiliation justice was denied Him. Who can describe His generation? For His life is taken away from the earth. (Acts 8:32–33)

The Ethiopian asked Philip, "About whom, I ask you, does the prophet say this, about himself or about someone else?" (v. 34). We hear how Philip answered: "Then Philip opened his mouth, and beginning with this Scripture he told him the good news about Jesus" (v. 35).

Suddenly, something peculiar happened. As Philip and the Ethiopian continued to travel, the Ethiopian saw water. The text tells us what happened next:

> The eunuch said, "See, here is water! What prevents me from being baptized?" And he commanded the chariot to stop, and they both went down into the water, Philip and the eunuch, and he baptized him. (vv. 36–38)

Why was the Ethiopian so insistent on being baptized? What was included in the "good news about Jesus" that created an urgency and craving in the Ethiopian for Baptism? Events recorded earlier in Acts give us a clue.

After the risen Jesus ascended into heaven, His disciples huddled in a house, waiting and wondering about Jesus' promise. Luke, the author of the Book of Acts, recounted the events:

> And while staying with them He ordered them not to depart from Jerusalem, but to wait for the promise of the Father, which, He said, "you heard from Me; for John baptized with water, but you will be baptized with the Holy Spirit not many days from now." (Acts 1:4–5)

Then Jesus told them, "You will receive power when the Holy Spirit has come upon you, and you will be My witnesses in Jerusalem and in all Judea and Samaria, and to the end of the earth" (v. 8).

So the disciples waited. Then, on the day of Pentecost, a harvest festival for the Jewish people, the sound of a rushing wind came from heaven and filled the house where they were gathered. Tongues of fire appeared on each of their heads, and they began to speak in all the languages of the people who were gathered there from many nations. People were astounded. But more than mere astonishment filled their hearts and minds. After the apostle Peter recapped how Jesus had been rejected, tortured, and killed, and yet rose from the dead as the true Messiah, the listeners were "cut to the heart," and they cried out to the disciples, "What shall we do?" (Acts 2:37).

The expression of need and urgency is similar to the Ethiopian's in Acts 8. That outcry for something more, for a deeper connection to make life complete, echoes in our hearts and lives. What shall we do when we fail? What shall we do when this life isn't enough? What shall we do when we're helpless? Peter responded:

> Repent and be baptized every one of you in the name of Jesus Christ for the forgiveness of your sins, and you

will receive the gift of the Holy Spirit. For the promise is for you and for your children and for all who are far off, everyone whom the Lord our God calls to Himself. (Acts 2:38–39)

The answer was in God's work, in His reach into life, in His miraculous and supernatural response to a fallen and broken world, where no answer can be found. The answer was in turning away from the old and tired ways of the world, the sinful and self-serving solutions of this life, and being returned to God's ways by the power of the Holy Spirit. Repentance is a gift of God. The apostle Paul told Timothy that God grants repentance (2 Timothy 2:25). The apostles proclaimed about Jesus, "God exalted Him at His right hand as Leader and Savior, to give repentance to Israel and forgiveness of sins" (Acts 5:31). After believers heard about Peter's experience with newly believing Gentiles, they exclaimed, "Then to the Gentiles also God has granted repentance that leads to life" (Acts 11:18). God gives the gift of repentance. He reaches into our stubborn lives and turns us around. While we are dead in our sins, God makes us alive in Jesus Christ (Ephesians 2:5).

He also makes a deep and abiding connection with us through Baptism. After Peter urged the people to be baptized, "those who received his word were baptized, and there were added that day about three thousand souls" (Acts 2:41). That's why the Ethiopian craved Baptism after he heard the Gospel message. It was God's way of bringing him the forgiveness of sins and the gift of the Holy Spirit. It was the supernatural connection that brought wholeness and life. It was a simple washing with water that cleansed deep into the soul.

Does God reach into our lives today? Does He close the mouths of the "lions" of guilt, meaninglessness, sin, and death? Does He make a connection with us that is tangible and sure, one that can serve as a reference point and foundation as we navigate the potentially brutal journey of life? He does, through the miraculous blessing of Baptism.

The apostle Paul experienced this miracle. You may remember that Paul was once called "Saul." He was a zealous Pharisee and was opposed to anyone who followed Jesus. When Stephen was put to death because of his confession of Jesus as the Christ, Scripture tells us the people killing Stephen "laid down their garments at the feet of a young man named Saul" (Acts 7:58). We also hear in Acts 8:1, "And Saul approved of [Stephen's] execution." But this was just the beginning. Acts 9 describes the heart and action of Saul:

> But Saul, still breathing threats and murder against the
> disciples of the Lord, went to the high priest and asked
> him for letters to the synagogues at Damascus, so that
> if he found any belonging to the Way, men or women,
> he might bring them bound to Jerusalem. (vv. 1–2)

Saul was on a mission of destruction. But Jesus stopped him in his tracks. As Saul traveled to Damascus, a bright light from heaven caused him to fall to the ground. Jesus' voice from heaven asked, "Saul, Saul, why are you persecuting Me?" (v. 4). Jesus told Saul, now blinded by the bright light, to get up and go into Damascus, where he would receive further instructions.

In the meantime, Jesus called to a disciple in Damascus named Ananias. Jesus told him, "Rise and go to the street called Straight, and at the house of Judas look for a man of Tarsus named Saul, for behold, he is praying, and he has seen in a vision a man named

Ananias come in and lay his hands on him so that he might regain his sight" (vv. 11–12). Ananias was understandably hesitant to pay a visit to Saul. Saul's reputation for brutality and harm was well known. The reason for his visit to Damascus was also understood by every Christian in the city. Saul was not the person any Christian wanted to cross paths with in Damascus. But Jesus persuaded Ananias to go by saying, "Go, for he is a chosen instrument of Mine to carry My name before the Gentiles and kings and the children of Israel. For I will show him how much he must suffer for the sake of My name" (vv. 15–16). God had a unique plan in store, so Ananias went.

Then we hear Ananias describe what God had commanded him to do. As he laid his hands on Saul, Ananias said to him, "Brother Saul, the Lord Jesus who appeared to you on the road by which you came has sent me so that you may regain your sight and be filled with the Holy Spirit" (v. 17). Notice the two jobs Jesus gave Ananias to accomplish: first, to restore Saul's sight; second, to make sure Saul was filled with the Holy Spirit. So, as Ananias's hands were upon Saul, "immediately something like scales fell from his eyes, and he regained his sight" (v. 18). Mission number one accomplished. Saul was physically healed. What about mission number two, the filling of the Holy Spirit? Verse 18 continues, "Then he rose and was baptized." Mission number two accomplished. How? With the gift of Baptism.

Saul didn't go through instruction classes. He wasn't asked if he wanted to confess his faith publicly. He wasn't taken to a river or lake to show the believers in Damascus that he was the real deal. Right then and there in a house in Damascus, God reached into Saul's corrupt and confused heart to fill him with the Holy

Spirit by means of a miraculous washing of grace. Whatever had fueled Saul's frenetic quest for recognition and meaning was finally quenched with God's gift of a new beginning through Baptism. Ordinary water applied in the name of the Father, Son, and Holy Spirit connected Saul to God's miraculous, forgiving, and new-life-giving reach into our lives.

A lions' den couldn't stop God. Neither could a Pharisee determined to destroy Him. Neither can the obstacles in your life. God turns you around and establishes a profound and meaningful connection with you through the blessing of Baptism.

BAPTISM

The word *baptism* in the New Testament means "to apply water, to wash." The verb *bapto* in the Greek translation of the Old Testament meant "to dip." Priests dipped their fingers in blood for sacrifices (Leviticus 4:6, 17). The feet of priests who carried the ark of the covenant were dipped into the Jordan River as they began to cross (Joshua 3:15). Naaman dipped himself seven times in the Jordan so he could be healed (*baptizo*, 2 Kings 5:14).

Two images come to mind when the word *baptism* is used. First, there is a cleansing, a washing that occurs. Second, there is a drowning, a perishing of the old and a birth of the new. During Bible times, people were very familiar with religious washings. When King Solomon built the temple, he included vessels for washing:

> He also made ten basins in which to wash, and set five
> on the south side, and five on the north side. In these
> they were to rinse off what was used for the burnt
> offering, and the sea was for the priests to wash in.
> (2 Chronicles 4:6)

Ceremonial washings called "baptisms" were very common in Judaism. Scripture notes the washing tradition of the Pharisees:

> For the Pharisees and all the Jews do not eat unless they wash their hands properly, holding to the tradition of the elders, and when they come from the marketplace, they do not eat unless they wash. And there are many other traditions that they observe, such as the washing of cups and pots and copper vessels and dining couches. (Mark 7:3–4)

The Greek words *bapto* and *baptizo* were known in New Testament times as washings that caused cleansing from impurity so the items washed could be used in service to God.[2] So, when people heard John the Baptist talk about "a baptism of repentance for the forgiveness of sins" (Luke 3:3–4), they understood what the word *baptism* was about. It was a washing that created holiness, a cleansing that produced a new condition before God.

The word *baptism* can be a bit more unfamiliar and strange during our time. The word has become a "church word," a ritual connected to a variety of meanings and interpretations. But the original use was power-packed with the mystery of God. When Baptism for repentance and forgiveness came on the scene, it became a lifeline for people to receive a new beginning, to be connected with the Holy God as He reached into broken and needy lives.

It is the connection we crave—given by God, in His grace, as a gift.

The power of baptism was even recognized by early followers of Judaism. When non-Jews were converted to Judaism, they were washed—baptized. It wasn't a symbol of a person becoming a Jew. The Jewish people saw it as an actual transformation. The person became a Jew through baptism. In fact, because female converts could not be circumcised as male converts were, the baptizing of Jewish converts became a standard procedure to transform a non-Jew into a true Jew. The baptizing even took place prior to Torah education. Baptism was considered a change agent that prepared the convert for instruction. This pre-Christian usage of baptism caused the early Greek meaning of the word for "baptism" to take on a transformative meaning.[3]

That's one of the reasons the Early Church began to baptize families, adults, and infants. Baptism was God doing His work, imparting His grace and Spirit on fallen and helpless people. We see examples of household Baptisms in Acts:

> One who heard us was a woman named Lydia, from the city of Thyatira, a seller of purple goods, who was a worshiper of God. The Lord opened her heart to pay attention to what was said by Paul. And after she was baptized, and her household as well, she urged us, saying, "If you have judged me to be faithful to the Lord, come to my house and stay." And she prevailed upon us. (16:14–15)

> And the jailer called for lights and rushed in, and trembling with fear he fell down before Paul and Silas. Then he brought them out and said, "Sirs, what must I do to be saved?" And they said, "Believe in the Lord Jesus, and you will be saved, you and your household." And they spoke the word of the Lord to him and to all

who were in his house. And he took them the same hour of the night and washed their wounds; and he was baptized at once, he and all his family. (vv. 29–34)

Just as Baptism was part of the saving news of Jesus for the Ethiopian, it was part of the key message of God's reach of grace for Lydia, the jailer, and their families.

This is when people start to get concerned, however. They ask, "So, just because someone is baptized, they get a 'free ticket' to heaven? What about a life of faith?"

It's a good question. But from the beginning, Baptism was not considered a "free ticket" to heaven, a check mark on a spiritual to-do list that guaranteed a heavenly roster spot whether you walked in faith or not. Baptism imparted all of God's gifts, but a person could still reject the Savior. People could walk away from His grace. That did not invalidate the Baptism. It simply meant that, tragically, an individual decided to push the Holy Spirit away.

Is the powerful and transforming gift of Baptism "cheap grace"? In other words, shouldn't there be some requirements that a person fulfills or some proof of commitment to Christ before Baptism happens? The Bible addresses this fear as it teaches about Baptism and the will of God for our lives. When Jesus gave the Great Commission, He told His followers how to make disciples: by baptizing and teaching. After Paul was baptized, he went immediately into Arabia for three years to study and learn what God wanted to teach him. He was discipled. Over and over again, the Bible urges us to grow in the knowledge of our Lord Jesus Christ and to grow in lives that are conformed to His image. Baptism is not a "free ticket" to heaven in the sense that once you get that stamp of approval, you can do anything you want and still hold on to your heaven guarantee. But it is a free ticket in the sense that the fullness of God's grace is poured into your life through Baptism. You receive the certainty of the life and salvation that the Holy Spirit gives. The calling that remains is to live in your Baptism—not apart from it. So when people who are old enough to speak are baptized, they're asked about their commitment to Christ and His teaching. When people who can't speak yet are baptized, their sponsors and parents are asked about the commitment to raise the child in faith. A free gift is not necessarily a "cheap" gift.

MYSTERY CRAVED AND GIVEN

We live in a strange time. On one hand, people are searching for meaning beyond what this world offers. There is a craving for fulfillment and connections that cannot be found in this temporal sphere of existence. On the other hand, mystery is spurned as unsophisticated and unscientific. If it can't be duplicated in the lab, it must not be true. We create a catch-22 by rejecting the very thing we need the most. Instead of looking to the accessible connection we've been given by God, our world urges us to dig deeply into our inner strength. Our create-your-own-destiny world would have advised Daniel to figure out how to manage those hungry lions.

But when God clears the fog of our controlling and self-centered inclinations, we being to rejoice in His miraculous reach. I remember a young lady named Chelsea. A friend invited her to come to a midweek youth ministry event at our church. Chelsea was an artistic and articulate girl. She had fun with the students who participated in our youth ministry. And she heard the Good News of a Savior in Jesus for the very first time. After she heard about Baptism, she began to *crave* it. She begged her parents to let her be baptized. She asked me to help get her baptized as soon as possible. Why? Like the Ethiopian and the families in the Book of Acts, she wanted God and His gifts in her life. So, very soon after she asked, Chelsea was baptized as her friends and family celebrated.

It was just like the celebrations of Baptism in the New Testament. The apostle Paul expressed his very personal knowledge in the special power of Baptism when he said, "Do you not know that all of us who have been baptized into Christ Jesus were baptized into His death? We were buried therefore with Him by baptism into death, in order that, just as Christ was raised from the dead by the glory of the Father, we too might walk in newness of life" (Romans 6:3–4).

God is full of surprises. He still reaches out to us and amazes us with His grace.

Michael Drysch was a fifty-year-old computer programmer when he got a chance to sink a half-court shot at a Miami Heat basketball game. If he made the shot, he would win $75,000. Knowing in advance that he had this chance, he practiced during the two days before the halftime challenge. He only got the ball in the hoop one time. Game time came. Drysch stretched his arm and wound up for a hook shot with twenty thousand people watching. The ball went up . . . and through the hoop! Suddenly, Miami Heat star LeBron James ran onto the court and tackled Michael Drysch in celebration. Smiling, shouting, and celebrating, James rolled on the floor with a shocked and delighted Drysch. Who would have ever thought that an ordinary computer programmer would be wrestling with a basketball superstar midcourt in an NBA arena?[4]

In Baptism, God runs out onto the court of your life, tackles you, and rolls around in celebration of the forgiveness of your sins and your new life in Jesus Christ—no basketball shot needed. Who would have thought that God would enter into our ordinary lives so easily, so graciously, and so beneficially? But the God who closed the mouths of lions still steps into our lives today through the washing called Baptism. That's what Jesus intended when He said:

> Go therefore and make disciples of all nations, baptizing them in the name of the Father and of the Son and of the Holy Spirit, teaching them to observe all that I have commanded you. And behold, I am with you always, to the end of the age. (Matthew 28:19–20)

The Savior who is with us provides the deep connection we crave. Who wouldn't celebrate such a blessed new beginning?

Notes

1. www.seattlepi.com/local/article/Grizzly-mauls-kills-a-bear-expert-1126392.php; en.wikipedia.org/wiki/Timothy_Treadwell; www.yellowstone-bearman.com/Tim_Treadwell.html

2. Gerhard Kittel, ed., *Theological Dictionary of the New Testament* (Grand Rapids: Eerdmans, 1968), vol. 1, 535.

3. Kittel, 536.

4. www.usatoday.com/story/gameon/2013/01/25/lebron-james-tackle-fan-half-court-video/1865811/

5. Paul McCain, ed., *Concordia: The Lutheran Confessions*, second edition (St. Louis: Concordia Publishing House, 2006), 424.

6. McCain, 424–25.

7. McCain, 425.
8. McCain, 425.
9. McCain, 427.
10. McCain, 427.

Read Exodus 3:7–8. This is a classic example of the way God works. He comes down to save us. He steps in. As he discussed Baptism, Martin Luther emphasized this action of God: "To be baptized in God's name is to be baptized not by men, but by God Himself. Therefore, although it is performed by human hands, it is still truly God's own work."[5]

1. Discuss how the true meaning of God's grace is seen in Daniel's experience in the den of lions and in the gift of Baptism.

2. Read Acts 22:12–16. The apostle Paul was telling his story to a crowd in Jerusalem. What did he tell the crowd his Baptism did for him?

3. How is it possible that Baptism connects people to God and gives people a new beginning? Read the following quote from Martin Luther to help you begin your discussion: "Baptism is quite a different thing from all other water. This is not because of its natural quality but because something more noble is added here. God Himself stakes His honor, His power, and His might on it."[6]

Baptism is called a "sacrament." A *sacrament* is defined as an action commanded by Jesus, connected to the promise of the forgiveness of sins, using a visible means or object. Martin Luther commented in his Large Catechism, "When the Word is added, as God has ordained, it is a Sacrament. It is called Christ's Baptism.

Let this be the first part about the holy Sacrament's essence and dignity."[7]

4. Why is this Sacrament so important, especially in light of the current condition of our culture and world? Discuss what needs it meets and how it stands in contrast to what the world offers.

Read Mark 16:16. Martin Luther commented on this verse: "Therefore, state it most simply in this way: the power, work, profit, fruit, and purpose of Baptism is this—to save [1 Peter 3:21]. For no one is baptized in order that he may become a prince, but, as the words say, that he 'be saved.' We know that to be saved is nothing other than to be delivered from sin, death, and the devil [Colossians 1:13–14]. It means to enter into Christ's kingdom [John 3:5], and to live with Him forever."[8]

5. Discuss how you and the world as you know it need to be saved at this time in history.

Read Galatians 3:26–28. Regarding Baptism, Martin Luther commented: "So you see plainly that there is no work done here by us, but a treasure, which God gives us and faith grasps [Ephesians 2:8–9]. It is like the benefit of the Lord Jesus Christ upon the cross, which is not a work, but a treasure included in the Word. It is offered to us and received by faith. Therefore, the 'new spirits' violate us by shouting against us as though we preach against faith. For we alone insist upon it as being so necessary that without it nothing can be received or enjoyed."[9]

6. What does it mean to be "clothed with Christ"?

7. Read Colossians 2:8–12. How do the warning and the promise Paul gives in these verses apply to your life?

8. Read Titus 3:3–7. Describe the way the work of Jesus and Baptism are connected. According to these verses, what blessings come through Baptism?

Martin Luther discussed how Baptism can be used by Christians every day: "We must think this way about Baptism and make it profitable for ourselves. So when our sins and conscience oppress us, we strengthen ourselves and take comfort and say, 'Nevertheless, I am baptized. And if I am baptized, it is promised to me that I shall be saved and have eternal life, both in soul and body.'"[10]

9. Talk about how living in your Baptism can provide strength to you as you face specific challenges and temptations in your life.

SEVEN

> "Take, eat; this is My body. . . . Drink of it, all of you, for this is My blood of the covenant, which is poured out for many for the forgiveness of sins." Matthew 26:26–28

YOUR PROVISION FOR THE JOURNEY

GOD IN THE DANCE

I'll never forget the wonderful expression of love and sacrifice I witnessed at a Girl Scout father-daughter sock hop. It was a while back, when my oldest daughter was a Daisy Girl Scout. Here she was, in kindergarten, nervous about her first dance and a little shy about the whole fifties dress-up thing. We walked into the school gym and what a sight it was! Grown men with hair slicked back, wearing white T-shirts with sleeves rolled up, black shoes on with white socks shining from beneath their rolled-up jean cuffs. The only thing that could get a guy to dress up like that was the little girl in the poodle skirt who gave him that "Daddy, I've got you in the palm of my hand" smile.

Throughout the night, these dads were shimmying and shaking, doing the hand jive and twirling their precious partners on the dance floor. Love led them to be in the dance.

If a dad didn't have time or didn't care or didn't want to be embarrassed, he wouldn't be there. When there is no love or when love is lacking, there isn't going to be much participation or presence. In the Bible, on the night Jesus gave the gift of Communion,

Judas was the man of separation and betrayal. The Bible shows how Judas was not in the dance. He went out into the darkness on his own.

This rejection of Jesus by Judas is just one ripple in the pond that started back in the Garden of Eden when Adam and Eve went off on their own in sin. And the ripples continue today when we go off on our own without the love of Jesus, trying to leave Him behind.

What is God's reaction? Well, to His fragile, hurting, broken, rebellious, and, yes, even ornery children, God stretches out His hand and says, "I want to be with you in the dance of life." The Bible makes it clear that He's always had this love and this heart for His children. From day one, God expressed His love through participation and presence. During the good days before the fall into sin, God was in the dance, walking in the garden and talking with His dear children. After people strayed, God was in the dance, appearing to Moses and delivering His people. When the people were in the wilderness, God was in the dance, guarding them with a pillar of fire and a pillar of cloud. When they worshiped, God was in the dance, filling the tabernacle with His glory, showing them that He was with them. When the people rebelled against God, He was in the dance, speaking and acting through prophets. At the right time, for the sin of the whole world, God was in the dance, sending His one and only Son, Jesus, to live for you and to die on the cross for you. And when Jesus was getting ready to leave this earth, which would happen after His death and resurrection, He told His disciples that He would stay in the dance. So they gathered for the Passover meal. Jesus took the bread and said, "Take and eat, this is My body." He took the cup of wine and said, "Drink from it, all of you, this is My blood." Jesus let the disciples know that the next time they would feast together would be in heaven. But for here and now, He was in the dance.

God's love and commitment to your life always means His participation and presence. The Meal Jesus instituted that night before His death is an extension of what God has always done. Some people say, "How could Jesus really be present when you eat and drink the bread and wine? How can the infinite God take up such lowly forms here and now?" Well, it was God's idea. It was His idea to slick His hair back, roll up His jeans, and dance with His children—always there, always forgiving, always strengthening. What would cause a grown God to do a thing like that? It's love that leads our Lord and Savior to be in the dance. And to have such a dance partner is something we crave deeply. You and I can't dance alone, and by God's grace, we don't have to.

Daniel discovered that as he traveled the difficult journey of captivity in Babylon. Along the way, God stepped in to help him time and time again. In Daniel 1, God gave Daniel and his friends favor in the eyes of guards. In chapter 2, God revealed the mystery of Nebuchadnezzar's dream in a vision. In chapter 3, the angel of the Lord appeared in the fiery furnace to save Shadrach, Meshach, and Abednego, and to cause a proclamation to the world that no god could ever save and rescue like the God of the three boys from Jerusalem. In chapter 6, God sent His angel to close the mouths of lions. Over and over again, God stepped in. He entered the dance of life to rescue and encourage Daniel and his friends.

As I mentioned earlier, however, the reign of Nebuchadnezzar's successor, Belshazzar, was a time of struggle for Daniel. Chapter 5 tells us only about the last days of Belshazzar's twenty-year reign.

Was God silent for two decades as Daniel was looked down upon and cast aside? Or did He enter "the dance" to help and encourage Daniel during this trying time?

The visions in the final chapters of the Book of Daniel give us an answer. Chapter 7 begins this way: "In the first year of Belshazzar king of Babylon, Daniel saw a dream and visions of his head as he lay in his bed. Then he wrote down the dream and told the sum of the matter" (v. 1). Chapter 8 recounts another one of Daniel's visions. This time the vision was given to Daniel in the third year of King Belshazzar's reign. It's important to realize that the visions in the Book of Daniel took place throughout Daniel's stay in Babylon. While they're grouped together in chapters 7–12, the visions came to Daniel over the course of a number of years as he served each king who came into power during the long captivity in Babylon. While the meaning of each vision is important, the fact that God reached out to Daniel at all is of great significance. During a challenging time under a ruler who seemed to forget about Daniel, God stepped in to encourage the captive prophet and to let him know that he was neither forgotten nor forsaken. He was given the provision of God's presence for the long journey of service to a ruler who did not seem to regard him highly.

The contents of the visions were alarming to Daniel, but each brought messages of encouragement. The vision in chapter 7 describes the rise and fall of successive earthly kingdoms, from the Babylonian kingdom to the Roman Empire. Trumping the power of these earthly dominions was the triumph of the Ancient of Days and One who looked like "a son of man." Daniel recounted:

> I saw in the night visions, and behold, with the clouds
> of heaven there came one like a son of man, and He

came to the Ancient of Days and was presented before
Him. And to Him was given dominion and glory and
a kingdom, that all peoples, nations, and languages
should serve Him; His dominion is an everlasting dominion, which shall not pass away, and His kingdom
one that shall not be destroyed. (vv. 13–14)

Daniel was given a glimpse of God's eternal victory and the
reign of His Son, Jesus, the Messiah. As Daniel sat in captivity and
wondered if God would ever reign again, the prophet was given
supernatural encouragement that all would be well—even when
evil tyrants seemed to be winning the day.

Chapter 8 brings a vision that was even more disturbing. A
wicked king would seek to destroy the people of God. He would
meet with some success and would desecrate the temple of God.
The angel Gabriel shared this message about the future with Daniel. After experiencing the vision, Daniel said:

And I, Daniel, was overcome and lay sick for some
days. Then I rose and went about the king's business,
but I was appalled by the vision and did not understand it. (v. 27)

But Daniel knew he wasn't alone. He knew that God had not
forgotten about him. In fact, God entrusted Daniel with a message about the future. It was not a burden Daniel wanted to bear,
but the message showed that God was "in the dance" with Daniel. The Most High God was close by. Daniel was not alone. And
God kept the contact going. In the first year of Darius's rule, Daniel
hoped for deliverance based on Jeremiah's prophecy that captivity
in Babylon would last for seventy years. Nearly seventy years had

already passed, so Daniel prayed a beautiful prayer of repentance. He confessed the collective sin of God's people. He praised God. He worshiped. Daniel's closing petitions capture the spirit of his plea to God:

> Now therefore, O our God, listen to the prayer of Your servant and to his pleas for mercy, and for Your own sake, O Lord, make Your face to shine upon Your sanctuary, which is desolate. O my God, incline Your ear and hear. Open Your eyes and see our desolations, and the city that is called by Your name. For we do not present our pleas before You because of our righteousness, but because of Your great mercy. O Lord, hear; O Lord, forgive. O Lord, pay attention and act. Delay not, for Your own sake, O my God, because Your city and Your people are called by Your name. (9:17–19)

Daniel prayed for God's mercy. While the prophet never experienced the blessing of being able to go home, God showed mercy by continually drawing close to His servant Daniel. The encouragement kept coming.

Even when the seventy years of captivity seemed to be completed, God did not keep silent. In the third year of the rule of the Medo-Persian Empire under Darius, Daniel received yet another detailed vision about future kingdoms and the end of time. Though the visions were astonishing and filled with mystery, Daniel was given the assurance, "Go your way till the end. And you shall rest and shall stand in your allotted place at the end of the days" (12:13). The prophet would not be abandoned in death, but would rise to life with God forever. God would stay in the dance with Daniel for eternity.

God's M.O.

That is how God works. It's His M.O., His "modus operandi" or "method of operation." If you've watched any detective or police shows, you know the term refers to the way a suspect works. Certain criminals always had ways of doing things. One bank robber would always wear a mask that looked like a U.S. president. A certain burglar would always eat a few goodies from his victims' refrigerators. A particular arsonist would always leave traces of the same chemicals. That was the M.O.

God has an M.O. too. He has a method of operation—not to do evil, but to bestow His grace in our lives. Over the centuries, God has shown that He works in a consistent and beautiful way. He draws close to us. He enters our existence. His modus operandi has been called "incarnational" and "sacramental." The Bible shows us that God has decided to be **present** with us for the **purpose of life and salvation**. In our broken and challenging journey, we, like Daniel, need God to draw near. In our "captivity" this side of heaven, we crave the saving closeness of God.

The Bible offers instance after instance of God's consistent M.O. In Exodus 3, we hear about Moses' encounter with the burning bush:

> Now Moses was keeping the flock of his father-in-law, Jethro, the priest of Midian, and he led his flock to the west side of the wilderness and came to Horeb, the mountain of God. And the angel of the LORD appeared to him in a flame of fire out of the midst of a bush. He looked, and behold, the bush was burning, yet it was not consumed. And Moses said, "I will turn aside to see this great sight, why the bush is not burned." When

the LORD saw that he turned aside to see, God called to him out of the bush, "Moses, Moses!" And he said, "Here I am." Then He said, "Do not come near; take your sandals off your feet, for the place on which you are standing is holy ground." And He said, "I am the God of your father, the God of Abraham, the God of Isaac, and the God of Jacob." And Moses hid his face, for he was afraid to look at God. Then the LORD said, "I have surely seen the affliction of My people who are in Egypt and have heard their cry because of their taskmasters. I know their sufferings, and I have come down to deliver them out of the hand of the Egyptians and to bring them up out of that land to a good and broad land, a land flowing with milk and honey." (vv. 1–8)

If you were to stop the action that day, tap Moses on the shoulder, and ask what was going on, what do you think he would say? Would he respond, "Well, I'm just interacting with a symbol of the God I love and trust. This moment provides me with an intimate spiritual experience for my personal growth and strength"? Is that what Moses would say? Or would he say, "See that bush? It's God! He's right here. You better take off your shoes and fall on your face in the presence of the Holy Lord."

Moses was talking to God—God who was **present** for the **purpose of saving His people**.

Later in the Book of Exodus, the people of Israel were freed by God's mighty and miraculous work. That's when they found themselves cornered—backed up to the raging Red Sea:

But God led the people around by the way of the wilderness toward the Red Sea. And the people of Israel went up out of the land of Egypt equipped for battle. ... And the LORD went before them by day in a pillar of cloud to lead them along the way, and by night in a pillar of fire to give them light, that they might travel by day and by night. The pillar of cloud by day and the pillar of fire by night did not depart from before the people. (13:18, 21–22)

Then the angel of God who was going before the host of Israel moved and went behind them, and the pillar of cloud moved from before them and stood behind them, coming between the host of Egypt and the host of Israel. And there was the cloud and the darkness. And it lit up the night without one coming near the other all night. Then Moses stretched out his hand over the sea, and the LORD drove the sea back by a strong east wind all night and made the sea dry land, and the waters were divided. And the people of Israel went into the midst of the sea on dry ground, the waters being a wall to them on their right hand and on their left. (14:19–22)

What if you were able to interview an Israelite during these exciting events? What if you asked him, "What is that pillar of cloud? And what about that pillar of fire?" Do you think the person traveling with the multitudes of former captives would reply, "Oh, those pillars are representations of the infinite and eternal God. When we see them, we are reminded about our deep and lasting connection with God above. We are brought closer to Him because of those beautiful illustrations of who He is in our lives"?

Is that what an Israelite would say? Or would he say, "That's God! Look, He's saving us from the Egyptians!"

Once again, we encounter God's gracious method of operation. God was present in those pillars. He was **present** for **the purpose of saving His people**.

Let's fast-forward to the tabernacle, that portable place of worship for God's people. As the people wandered in the wilderness, they still had a connection point with the eternal God. He came down to dwell with them, to relieve them of their burdens, and to cleanse them from their sin. Exodus 40 describes what happened in this elaborate worship tent:

> Then the cloud covered the tent of meeting, and the glory of the LORD filled the tabernacle. And Moses was not able to enter the tent of meeting because the cloud settled on it, and the glory of the LORD filled the tabernacle. Throughout all their journeys, whenever the cloud was taken up from over the tabernacle, the people of Israel would set out. But if the cloud was not taken up, then they did not set out till the day that it was taken up. For the cloud of the LORD was on the tabernacle by day, and fire was in it by night, in the sight of all the house of Israel throughout all their journeys. (vv. 34–38)

Shall we interview Moses or an Israelite again? I think you get the idea. The cloud was not viewed as a symbolic representation of God. It *was* God—God with His people! It was God's modus operandi—His **presence** for the **purpose of saving His people**.

The Bible recounts God's constant action of being present with

His people for their salvation. The prophets were not just men who spoke about God and His will. They were the embodiment of God's message. Why? For the purpose of saving His people.

God continued His method of operation in the wondrous events of Matthew 1:

> Now the birth of Jesus Christ took place in this way. When His mother Mary had been betrothed to Joseph, before they came together she was found to be with child from the Holy Spirit. And her husband Joseph, being a just man and unwilling to put her to shame, resolved to divorce her quietly. But as he considered these things, behold, an angel of the Lord appeared to him in a dream, saying, "Joseph, son of David, do not fear to take Mary as your wife, for that which is conceived in her is from the Holy Spirit. She will bear a son, and you shall call His name Jesus, for He will save His people from their sins." All this took place to fulfill what the Lord had spoken by the prophet: "Behold, the virgin shall conceive and bear a son, and they shall call His name Immanuel" (which means, God with us). (vv. 18–23)

Jesus was the **presence** of God for the **purpose of salvation**! Jesus was consistent with the M.O. God established at creation and reinforced throughout history.

Then, on the night Jesus was betrayed, Jesus said something to the disciples that is recounted four times in the Bible. The Gospel of Matthew tells it this way:

> Now as they were eating, Jesus took bread, and after

> blessing it broke it and gave it to the disciples, and said, "Take, eat; this is My body." And He took a cup, and when He had given thanks He gave it to them, saying, "Drink of it, all of you, for this is My blood of the covenant, which is poured out for many for the forgiveness of sins. I tell you I will not drink again of this fruit of the vine until that day when I drink it new with you in My Father's kingdom." (26:26–29)

There it is again, God's method of operation. Before Jesus left the earth, He made sure that God's method of interacting with His people would continue. Jesus provided His body and blood in Communion. He promised that it was given for the forgiveness of our sins. Once again, Jesus provided His **presence** for the **purpose of salvation** in what we know as the Lord's Supper. This unique and miraculous presence would tide us over until the day we celebrate the heavenly feast with God face-to-face.

God stayed "in the dance" even when the Son of God ascended into heaven.

What if you walked up to Jesus during the Last Supper and asked, "Isn't this really just a symbolic tool to connect us to You spiritually?"

I wonder if Jesus would reply, "Did you hear what I said? This is My body. This is My blood. It is My presence with you until we are reunited in heaven. That is how My Father has always worked. And that is how He will continue to work until the Last Day."

There are times you may feel alone, as Daniel did. You may feel hopeless as the condition of the world seems to get worse. But God provides connection points. He answers our craving for His real presence in order to strengthen us and let us know we are not alone. In the gift of common bread and wine attached to Jesus' promise, we find ourselves like Daniel did: reached by God in the turbulence of a raging and stormy world. How good it is that He comes to us.

It's true that the Lord's Supper—also called Holy Communion—can seem strange in our day and age. Meals in our culture are not as much about fellowship as they once were. Several years ago, a rabbi friend and I met for lunch fairly regularly. When we got together, he always told me that in order to have true fellowship, we needed to break bread together. A real relationship took place over a meal. These days, meals are more about fast than fellowship. Eating on the run, going through the drive-thru, and zapping a frozen dinner in the microwave define mealtime in America much more than the word *fellowship* does. Meals can be considered interruptions—necessary caloric intrusions into our very busy days.

On the opposite end of the spectrum, food has become a decadent tool for self-indulgence and entertainment. When cable television has a Food Network, you know that intimate relationships are not the goal. Commercialism has taken over! "Sinful" indulgence in succulent treats becomes a hobby for well-fed Americans or a method of escape from a stressful existence. The purpose of having a meal with others has gone through some startling changes.

But a meal in New Testament times was a high point of establishing and cultivating a relationship. Eating together was true fellowship. It involved time, conversation, honesty, and friendship. When someone was welcomed at the table, that person was considered a friend and equal, someone honored and cared for. So, on the night before His crucifixion, when Jesus provided a *meal*, it was an amazing and meaningful gift. It brought the blessing of lasting fellowship. It was the ultimate expression of being truly present. This was not the old Passover meal. This was a new covenant as Jesus promised to be truly present in the bread and wine—**present for the purpose of our salvation.** After all, when you look closely at God's track record, when you realize the way He has worked throughout time, when you see that He wants to continue working in our lives as He has throughout history, then the Lord's Supper makes much more sense. God is gracious enough to be tangible in our world. He refuses to be merely an idea. Beyond our cognitive apprehension of God, He gives us His tangible presence for the purpose of our salvation.

THE DEATH PRINCIPLE

But is Jesus *really* present in the Lord's Supper?

An interesting biblical teaching tells us that the answer is a resounding yes.

I call it "the death principle."

The apostle Paul ran into challenges regarding the Lord's Supper. The challenges weren't expressed in theological arguments, but were seen in the careless administration of the Lord's Supper. In 1 Corinthians 11, Paul expressed dismay over what was happening during the worship services of that congregation:

> But in the following instructions I do not commend you, because when you come together it is not for the better but for the worse. For, in the first place, when you come together as a church, I hear that there are divisions among you. And I believe it in part, for there must be factions among you in order that those who

are genuine among you may be recognized. When you come together, it is not the Lord's supper that you eat. For in eating, each one goes ahead with his own meal. One goes hungry, another gets drunk. What! Do you not have houses to eat and drink in? Or do you despise the church of God and humiliate those who have nothing? What shall I say to you? Shall I commend you in this? No, I will not. (vv. 17–22)

Paul then went on to describe exactly how the Lord's Supper should be approached:

For I received from the Lord what I also delivered to you, that the Lord Jesus on the night when He was betrayed took bread, and when He had given thanks, He broke it, and said, "This is My body which is for you. Do this in remembrance of Me." In the same way also He took the cup, after supper, saying, "This cup is the new covenant in My blood. Do this, as often as you drink it, in remembrance of Me." For as often as you eat this bread and drink the cup, you proclaim the Lord's death until He comes. Whoever, therefore, eats the bread or drinks the cup of the Lord in an unworthy manner will be guilty concerning the body and blood of the Lord. Let a person examine himself, then, and so eat of the bread and drink of the cup. For anyone who eats and drinks without discerning the body eats and drinks judgment on himself. (vv. 23–29)

What follows is an amazing statement that shows the Lord's real presence in Communion. As I mentioned, I call it "the death principle." In the Old Testament, we hear that coming into the presence of God as an unprepared, unconsecrated, or unrepentant sinner meant certain death. Exodus 28 provides a good example. Embedded in the instructions for Aaron's priestly garments and his entry into the Holy Place of the tabernacle, we read:

> Make pomegranates of blue, purple and scarlet yarn around the hem of the robe, with gold bells between them. The gold bells and the pomegranates are to alternate around the hem of the robe. Aaron must wear it when he ministers. The sound of the bells will be heard when he enters the Holy Place before the LORD and when he comes out, so that he will not die. (vv. 33–35 NIV)

Notice that if Aaron entered the presence of God unprepared, he would die. This was a principle God communicated to His people a number of times. No sinner could come into the presence of the Holy God and live. The apostle Paul underscored this principle when he said to the Church in Corinth, "For anyone who eats and drinks without discerning the body eats and drinks judgment on himself. That is why many of you are weak and ill, and some have died" (1 Corinthians 11:29–30).

Unrepentant sinners were carelessly partaking in the Lord's Supper. They came into the presence of God unprepared and unconsecrated. They did not recognize the body of Christ. So, harm resulted. Some became sick and weak. Others died. Clearly, the people of Corinth did not merely come into contact with something in their spiritual imaginations. This was not an encounter with a recollection. These people did not suffer the consequences of a symbolic representation in the Lord's Supper. Symbols do not cause death. Only the presence of God—His presence for the purpose of salvation—could cause such results.

"The death principle" underscores the startling gravity and wonder of God connecting with us through the bread and wine in the Lord's Supper. It's a wonderful gift. Think about it: Jesus reaches into your life in a miraculous and mysterious way to fill you with His presence and impart the forgiveness of sins. This is something you and I need desperately. It is provision for life's arduous journey. It is a meal in which Jesus enters into our lives in order to sustain us and renew us during our walk on this side of eternity. It is the Savior's real presence—miraculously with us for the purpose of our salvation.

The Lord's Supper and You

But how does the Lord's Supper work? How is Jesus present in the bread and wine?

The Bible mentions Jesus' institution of the Lord's Supper four times. In Matthew 26:26–29, we read:

> Now as they were eating, Jesus took bread, and after blessing it broke it and gave it to the disciples, and said, "Take, eat; this is My body." And He took a cup, and when He had given thanks He gave it to them, saying, "Drink of it, all of you, for this is My blood of the covenant, which is poured out for many for the forgiveness of sins. I tell you I will not drink again of this fruit of the vine until that day when I drink it new with you in My Father's kingdom."

Mark 14:22–25 tells us:

> And as they were eating, He took bread, and after blessing it broke it and gave it to them, and said, "Take; this is My body." And He took a cup, and when He had given thanks He gave it to them, and they all drank of it. And He said to them, "This is My blood of the covenant, which is poured out for many. Truly, I say to you, I will not drink again of the fruit of the vine until that day when I drink it new in the kingdom of God."

In Luke 22 it happens again:

> And He took bread, and when He had given thanks, He broke it and gave it to them, saying, "This is My body, which is given for you. Do this in remembrance of Me." And likewise the cup after they had eaten, saying, "This cup that is poured out for you is the new covenant in My blood." (vv. 19–20)

Then, in 1 Corinthians 11, we hear the apostle Paul teach new believers about one of the most important gifts Jesus gave:

> For I received from the Lord what I also delivered to you, that the Lord Jesus on the night when He was betrayed took bread, and when He had given thanks, He broke it, and said, "This is My body which is for you. Do this in remembrance of Me." In the same way also He took the cup, after supper, saying, "This cup is the new covenant in My blood. Do this, as often as you drink it, in remembrance of Me." For as often as you eat this bread and drink the cup, you proclaim the Lord's death until He comes. (vv. 23–26)

The repetition is significant. The Lord's Supper is not an auxiliary teaching of the New Testament. It's not a small and minor point that can be overlooked. It is an important gift. God wanted to make sure that we did not miss out on His miraculous reach into our lives through this special and gracious Meal. He wanted us to know that He was making a connection of grace for our lives in need. In 1 Corinthians 10, Paul underscored the presence of Jesus in Communion:

> The cup of blessing that we bless, is it not a participation in the blood of Christ? The bread that we break, is it not a participation in the body of Christ? (v. 16)

The emphasis of the importance of Communion is clear. The central point of that emphasis is the presence of the Son of God for the purpose of our salvation. Over and over again, we hear Jesus say, "This is My body. . . . This is My blood."

How does Communion work? The answer is simple: because Jesus said it does. It is part of the miraculous revelation of our heavenly Father. Like the burning bush, the pillars of cloud and fire, the smoke that filled the tabernacle, and the incarnate Son of God Himself, it is part of the remarkable reach of God into our lives. It is God doing His faithful and saving work until we eat and drink this feast with Him in heaven.

Do you crave this gift, this connection with God for your strength and new life? I hope so. In a world that seems to take us apart, run us ragged, and pull us away from God, Jesus comes to us in the Holy Meal He gave to put us back together, give us rest, and draw us close. How can you receive such a gift?

The first step is to note the biblical mandate to confess your sins and to confess faith in Jesus, your Savior. Acknowledging your sins happens privately and publicly. Recognizing your deep need for God's forgiveness begins in your own heart. It can be expressed privately to a Christian friend or to a pastor. It is also expressed publicly as, together with a community of faith, you confess your sins.

Another component of your preparation is acknowledging that the gift of Holy Communion is not a solo venture. It is for the community of believers—a public meal of fellowship. That's why the apostle Paul said to believers in Corinth:

> The cup of blessing that we bless, is it not a participation in the blood of Christ? The bread that we break, is it not a participation in the body of Christ? Because there is one bread, we who are many are one body, for we all partake of the one bread. Consider the people of Israel: are not those who eat the sacrifices participants in the altar? What do I imply then? That food offered to idols is anything, or that an idol is anything? No, I imply that what pagans sacrifice they offer to demons and not to God. I do not want you to be participants with demons. You cannot drink the cup of the Lord and the cup of demons. You cannot partake of the table of the Lord and the table of demons. Shall we provoke the Lord to jealousy? Are we stronger than He? "All things are lawful," but not all things are helpful. "All things are lawful," but not all things build up. Let no one seek his own good, but the good of his neighbor. (1 Corinthians 10:16–24)

Later, Paul adds:

So, whether you eat or drink, or whatever you do, do
all to the glory of God. Give no offense to Jews or to
Greeks or to the church of God, just as I try to please
everyone in everything I do, not seeking my own ad-
vantage, but that of many, that they may be saved. (vv.
31–33)

These verses address two issues. One is clearly about living a
divided life—the participation in pagan acts along with Christian
confession. That can't happen. In Corinth, it was causing other believers to stumble and weaken in their faith.

The second issue addressed is about the public nature of Communion. In addition to being a personal and restoring communion with the real presence of Jesus, it is also a communion with
fellow believers. It is a living out of community—an expression of
the oneness of faith. Communion is called "Communion" because
it has a corporate element. These days we want to individualize
everything we do. We devalue community. The Bible makes it clear
that participating in Communion impacts the faith community.
That's why Paul emphasized seeking the good of others and trying not to cause anyone to stumble. That is also why the Christian
Church through the ages has emphasized the biblical responsibilities surrounding Communion. Serving one another and giving
honor to Jesus are central to the Lord's Supper—all for our good
and the good of others. Baptized believers in Jesus who confess the
faith of a local congregation or a network of congregations come to
the Lord's Supper for God's blessing and forgiveness. Throughout
the Church, individual believers and Christian denominations respect the faith confession of others and try not to disrupt the unity
of fellow believers. It's not always easy to navigate these biblical

mandates, but it is always for the purpose of loving God and loving others.

And so, we are knit together with fellow believers in a spirit of self-sacrificial service. In this precious gift—this connection point with God—you confess a common faith and you are united in fellowship with the body of believers. You are brought from isolation to friendship. God's grace makes sure that you are no longer alone. It is His blessed and gracious provision for the journey of life. We crave God to be in the dance with us. In the Lord's Supper, He takes our hand and leads us in His gracious steps.

Notes

1. Paul McCain, ed., *Concordia: The Lutheran Confessions,* second edition (St. Louis: Concordia Publishing House, 2006), 434.

2. McCain, 432.

3. McCain, 439.

4. McCain, 440.

STUDY GUIDE FOR CHAPTER SEVEN

YOUR PROVISION FOR THE JOURNEY

1. God kept appearing to Daniel in his long and difficult captivity. How does God show up for you as you navigate the highs and lows of "the dance" called life?

Martin Luther commented about Communion: The Lord's Supper "is indeed called a food of souls, which nourishes and strengthens the new man. For by Baptism we are first born anew [John 3:5]. But, as we said before, there still remains the old vicious nature of flesh and blood in mankind. There are so many hindrances and temptations of the devil and of the world that we often become weary and faint, and sometimes we also stumble [Hebrews 12:3]. Therefore, the Sacrament is given as a daily pasture and sustenance, that faith may refresh and strengthen itself [Psalm 23:1–3] so that it will not fall back in such a battle, but become ever stronger and stronger."[1]

2. Discuss the importance of "daily sustenance" for your faith—what wears your faith down and what impact a "refreshed" faith has in your life.

3. The chapter covered several instances of God being present for the purpose of saving His people. What additional biblical instances of this "M.O." of God can you think of?

4. Why is God's modus operandi important for our lives today?

Holy Communion is another biblical sacrament. Jesus commanded it; He promised that it gives the forgiveness of sins; and it utilizes visible means: bread and wine. Martin Luther summarized what the Sacrament of Holy Communion is when he said, "It is the true body and blood of our Lord Jesus Christ, in and under the bread and wine, which we Christians are commanded by Christ's Word to eat and to drink."[2]

> 5. How does this meal containing the mystery of Christ meet a real need in our lives and world today?

In his Large Catechism, Martin Luther also commented on God's gracious invitation to partake of this healing meal: "If, therefore, you are heavy laden and feel your weakness, then go joyfully to this Sacrament and receive refreshment, comfort, and strength [Matthew 11:28]. If you wait until you are rid of such burdens, so that you might come to the Sacrament pure and worthy, you must stay away forever."[3]

> 6. These words are somewhat counterintuitive. We tend to feel that we must have our lives in complete order to receive Communion. What is Luther telling us and how are his statements reinforced by Jesus' words when He instituted Communion?

In his discussion about why we need to receive the Lord's Supper, Luther said, "Besides this, you will also have the devil about you. You will not entirely tread him under foot [Luke 10:19], because our Lord Christ Himself could not entirely avoid him. Now, what is the devil? Nothing other than what the Scriptures call him, a liar and a murderer [John 8:44]. He is a liar, to lead the heart astray from God's Word and to blind it, so that you cannot feel your distress or come to Christ. He is a murderer, who cannot bear to see you live one single hour. If you could see how many knives, darts, and arrows are every moment aimed at you [Ephesians 6:16], you would be glad to come to the Sacrament as often as possible."[4]

7. Luther brings up the reality of spiritual warfare. Read Ephesians 6:10–18. How is the spiritual armor in these verses fueled and reinforced by the gift of the Lord's Supper?

8. How do you personally prepare for the Lord's Supper?

9. Read John 6:35–51. Jesus isn't talking about Communion in these verses, but His conversation captures God's gracious work for us. What stands out to you in these verses regarding the grace of God and His persistent and caring reach into your life?

EIGHT

> "Go your way;
> behold, I am sending
> you out as lambs in
> the midst of wolves."
> Luke 10:3

YOUR BOLD MISSION

LAUNCHING

The mission sounds simple and seems exciting. Step 1: Use space travel technology and know-how to demonstrate the capability to land a spacecraft on the planet Mars. Step 2: Send a Mars rover vehicle to scout out the planet in order to find a good place to live. Step 3: Launch six rockets filled with housing and life-support units to be set up robotically on the planet. Final step: Send the first four people to Mars to start the first human Mars settlement. There's just one catch: if you're one of the new Mars dwellers, you can never return to earth, because the technology does not exist to bring you back.

That is what a business venture group called Mars One hopes to accomplish by the year 2025. It is a privately funded space exploration project and is actively recruiting twenty-four people for the one-way trip to Mars. Who would ever volunteer to leave earth's friendly environment to live on the harsh and foreboding red planet? Apparently, a very large number of people. The Mars One project received 200,000 applicants! More than one thousand made it to the short list and will begin testing for this permanent getaway.[1]

Why would people clamor to be a part of this risky undertaking? I think I know two answers. First, people become weary of life in this world. While there is great blessing and beauty on earth, it is not difficult to see our sense of hope becoming drained. Political corruption and arguments fill the airwaves. Wars rage on, plaguing nations and taking innocent lives. Violence runs rampant, victimizing the young and defenseless. Suffering seems to be out of control as disasters strike, economies crash, and illness ravages lives. As I wrote this book, news of a senseless murder hit the headlines. Just a few miles from where I live, a twenty-four-year-old graduate student was brutally murdered. She was jogging in a park in the late afternoon. It was still light outside. There were people in the park with her. But someone she'd never met confronted her and stabbed her to death. It was a senseless and heartbreaking death. The young lady had her heart set on helping people as she prepared to enter the medical field. She was a Christian who had been active in local and international mission trips. She was a loyal friend and a precious daughter. Imagine her parents' horrible shock and grief when police broke the news to them. If you've experienced violence directed toward a loved one, you know how agonizing it is to think about the pain, suffering, and thoughts in your loved one's final moments. These awful events take your breath away. The brutal and chaotic reality of a broken and sinful world creates unimaginable pain and drains away hope. Who wants to stay in such a world?

Add frantic busyness, the constant clamor of electronic devices, the overwhelming stress of multitasking, and endless pressure from responsibilities and worries, and the waiting list for Mars has the potential to grow very long. People need hope, and when hope is drained away by a relentlessly difficult world, they're ready to take a chance on another planet. It's sad, but true.

A second reason 200,000 people applied to take a one-way trip to Mars may be that we human beings crave a bold mission. We want to make a difference. It's difficult to live without a reason for existence. Even though routines can be nice and living comfortably can feel safe and secure, the need for significance and making an impact is crucial to human life. Whether it is raising a child, feeding the hungry, praying for ones in need, advancing the cause of a company, or providing for your family, a mission is essential. But isn't it true that the nature of life in our world drains mission? Challenges make us tired. We get too busy for big goals and dreams. We lose focus on the big picture as distractions send us scurrying in all directions. Pulled into maintenance and survival, we suffocate under a shortsighted, boring, and uninspiring existence.

But we know there is more to life. We crave a sense of meaning and a spirit of adventure. We know that God created us for a grand purpose. Even Jesus invited His disciples into an audacious calling. He led them away from the family fishing business and called them to be "fishers of men" (Matthew 4:19). He invited Peter to walk on water (Matthew 14:29). He gave the local boys from Galilee a big vision: "Go into all the world and proclaim the gospel to the whole creation" (Mark 16:15). Instead of leaving our lives in the futility and purposelessness of sin, Jesus gave the gift of a redeemed life with a mission.

But mission slowly seeps away as the world's promises of fulfillment are revealed as empty lies. So people line up for an even bigger adventure. They wonder if a trip to Mars can give them the bold mission that will finally satisfy.

Turning Inward

During his many years of captivity, Daniel could have wondered if there was something that would finally satisfy him. He couldn't go home, but could he find fulfillment in his home away from home? Should he give himself over to the ways of his captors? Should he surrender to the culture?

God answered Daniel's questions. In the final chapters of the Book of Daniel, visions of self-absorbed and self-exalting kings dominate. If Daniel had any internal inclination to abandon his walk with God and to align himself with the kings that kept him in captivity, God made sure that all such tempting illusions were cast aside as He showed Daniel the true character of the kings and their ultimate end. God taught Daniel that what appears to be mighty and in control may not endure. The vision in Daniel 11 provides clear and sobering lessons:

> Then a mighty king will arise, who will rule with great power and do as he pleases. After he has arisen, his kingdom will be broken up and parceled out toward the four winds of heaven. It will not go to his descendants, nor will it have the power he exercised, because his empire will be uprooted and given to others. (vv. 3–4 NIV)

> Then the king of the South will march out in a rage and fight against the king of the North, who will raise a large army, but it will be defeated. When the army is carried off, the king of the South will be filled with pride and will slaughter many thousands, yet he will not remain triumphant. (vv. 11–12 NIV)

> He will pitch his royal tents between the seas at the
> beautiful holy mountain. Yet he will come to his end,
> and no one will help him. (v. 45 NIV)

God revealed a progression of kings and kingdoms to Daniel. From the Persian Empire to Greece, Egypt, Syria, and Rome, God gave Daniel knowledge of kings, alliances, and battles of the future. Daniel could have easily lost hope as he saw the array of rulers placed before his eyes. Daniel could have given up on the mission of God as his captive experience dominated his life and it appeared that it would not come to an end before his death. But God provided what Daniel needed. God sustained Daniel both in hope and in mission. As Daniel wondered about visions that were too great for him to understand, God blessed him with an eternal perspective:

> At that time shall arise Michael, the great prince who
> has charge of your people. And there shall be a time of
> trouble, such as never has been since there was a na-
> tion till that time. But at that time your people shall be
> delivered, everyone whose name shall be found writ-
> ten in the book. And many of those who sleep in the
> dust of the earth shall awake, some to everlasting life,
> and some to shame and everlasting contempt. And
> those who are wise shall shine like the brightness of
> the sky above; and those who turn many to righteous-
> ness, like the stars forever and ever. (12:1–3)

> As for you, go your way till the end. You will rest, and
> then at the end of the days you will rise to receive your
> allotted inheritance. (v. 13 NIV)

The day was coming when all evil would be conquered for good. The day was coming when truth would emerge as the real winner. The day of deliverance and resurrection was coming. And God's redeemed people would shine like stars forever and ever.

While you may sometimes feel like hopping onto a spaceship to Mars, what you really need is hope and a mission. Fortunately, God gives both of those precious gifts to us. Even when everything seems like it's going wrong, God pours a heaping dose of hope into our lives. Even when we feel like we're defeated, God weaves His gracious mission into our fitful and imperfect existence. The apostle Paul expressed these precious gifts in a conversation with Christians in the city of Corinth: For God, who said, "Let light shine out of darkness," has shone in our hearts to give the light of the knowledge of the glory of God in the face of Jesus Christ. (2 Corinthians 4:6)

Note the gift of the light of Jesus!

> But we have this treasure in jars of clay, to show that the surpassing power belongs to God and not to us. We are afflicted in every way, but not crushed; perplexed, but not driven to despair; persecuted, but not forsaken; struck down, but not destroyed; always carrying in the body the death of Jesus, so that the life of Jesus may also be manifested in our bodies. For we who live are always being given over to death for Jesus' sake, so that the life of Jesus also may be manifested in our mortal flesh. So death is at work in us, but life in you. (vv. 7–12)

Note the beautiful mission of God—the proclamation of Jesus

even when we feel broken and overcome!

> Since we have the same spirit of faith according to what has been written, "I believed, and so I spoke," we also believe, and so we also speak, knowing that He who raised the Lord Jesus will raise us also with Jesus and bring us with you into His presence. For it is all for your sake, so that as grace extends to more and more people it may increase thanksgiving, to the glory of God. (vv. 13–15)

Note the power of the resurrection and the mission of extending the grace of God to more people!

> So we do not lose heart. Though our outer self is wasting away, our inner self is being renewed day by day. For this light momentary affliction is preparing for us an eternal weight of glory beyond all comparison, as we look not to the things that are seen but to the things that are unseen. For the things that are seen are transient, but the things that are unseen are eternal. (vv. 16–18)

Note the eternal perspective of hope—even when we suffer!

Daniel saw that he was not called to the empty ways of kings or to the hollow promises of the world. He was given eternal hope in his Savior. He was given a mission—not to be a "flash in the pan," but to shine like stars for eternity. Daniel's life is a good case study. Even though Daniel was displaced, God provided the life he craved—a life not alone, a life connected with God, and a life with the rich purpose of changing the world for the Most High God. This is the remarkable blessing you receive too. You're given the life you really crave—better than you can crave! You are given the eternal hope of Jesus Christ, the Savior who has won the victory over the most challenging enemy: death. And you are given a mission that doesn't end on a dusty red planet. You are given the privilege and honor of shining the light of Jesus so that the people around you can receive the best and most lasting blessing imaginable: new and eternal life in Jesus Christ.

A Bold Mission

This is what the world really needs. Contrary to popular opinion, the boldest mission around is not planning a multi-billion-dollar launch to Mars. It's not starting up a new company. It's not climbing a mountain or taking an African safari. The most daring mission involves what the world has difficulty doing: showing the radical love of Jesus and connecting people to eternal life. That's a bold mission because we have such a difficult time with it. We have a difficult time with people. I've heard it said—half in jest—"The church [or my job, my family, etc.] would be great if it weren't for the people." We screen calls, use the drive-thru, pay at the pump, and hide when the doorbell rings because people interrupt us, challenge us, and inconvenience us. We have a difficult time with people.

We can also be very mean to people. Bullying has always been a problem. The Cain-and-Abel incident in Genesis 4 displayed the human tendency to let cruelty run amok. Cyberbullying has sent too many young people into despair and self-destruction. Calling names, gossiping, excluding people, expressing prejudice, and doling out unkind words have damaged people's hearts and spirits across the course of time. In every circumstance, we can be very mean. We can inflict deep wounds upon God's precious children.

Bret Dunlap knows that. He was only six years old when he broke away from his big brothers to run across the street in order to catch a glimpse of his friend's new toy. The driver of the pickup truck didn't see him in the middle of the street as he came from around a blind curve. Bret was hit so hard, his shoes came off with his socks still in them. He slid over fifty feet before someone stopped him. A piece of the pickup's grill was embedded in his jacket. Miraculously, Bret lived. But in addition to several broken bones and internal injuries, he suffered severe brain damage. Doctors thought he would never survive. If he did, he would never walk or function. But through the tenacious love and hard work of his mother, Bret learned to walk. He learned to play the piano with the hand that still worked. He grew in knowledge and mastered his homework from school. Even though he couldn't say the answers as fast as the other kids, he knew them. His mother's love was tough. She never used the word *handicapped*. She said, "You can't do all the things the other kids do? Tough. You're going to have to deal with it." So Bret and his mom forged ahead.

They traveled through depression. They navigated medications. They sweated through physical therapy. Bret took college classes and got a job. He learned German and Latin. He studied history. He aspired to breeding chickens. He developed a dry sense of humor. He yearned for the loving embrace of a woman. But he couldn't express these things verbally. People around him became uncomfortable when he tried to talk, so he stopped trying. People were mean to him. They made fun of him. So he withdrew. He stayed out of people's way for over thirty years.

Then Bret's brother invited him to run a 5K race with him

in Rhinelander, Wisconsin. At first, Bret declined—not because he didn't think he could run the distance, but because he didn't want to make people uncomfortable. Bret's brother persisted until Bret finally agreed. That's when something amazing happened. Bret noticed that his fellow runners were being kind to him. They listened to him and didn't mind that he had difficulty speaking. They didn't criticize him because of his awkward gait. They welcomed him. So Bret kept running. He even completed a marathon.[2]

What brought Bret to such an amazing accomplishment? Love. The love of his mother, his brother, a boss who gave him a chance, and runners who welcomed him no matter how he looked or talked. Love lifted Bret out of feelings of inferiority, rejection, and pain. But love had to counter a powerful and awful force: hatred and meanness. Doctors called Bret "stupid." Teachers called him "slow." Kids were cruel. Adults counted him out. There was no shortage of outright cruelty. And the cruelty came from people just like you and me.

One of the most difficult things to do is to truly show love— self-sacrificial, sincere, constructive, selfless love. But that is what God did for us in a radical and entrepreneurial way. The apostle John declared, "This is love: not that we loved God, but that He loved us and sent His Son as an atoning sacrifice for our sins" (1 John 4:10 NIV). John went on to say, "Beloved, if God so loved us, we also ought to love one another" (v. 11). The apostle learned much from his Master. Jesus said to the disciples, "A new commandment I give to you, that you love one another: just as I have loved you, you also are to love one another. By this all people will know that you are My disciples, if you have love for one another" (John 13:34–35). This is where the bold mission of Jesus begins.

The apostle John learned this from experience. It is believed that John was the youngest of Jesus' disciples. He was James's little brother. I wonder if John got picked on. We don't know for sure, but there are incidents of wrangling among Jesus' disciples. Following the transfiguration of Jesus and the healing of a demon-possessed boy, we are told about a brouhaha that brewed among the disciples: "An argument arose among them as to which of them was the greatest" (Luke 9:46). Mark records the event, as well. He tells it this way:

> And they came to Capernaum. And when He was in the house He asked them, "What were you discussing on the way?" But they kept silent, for on the way they had argued with one another about who was the greatest. And He sat down and called the twelve. And He said to them, "If anyone would be first, he must be last of all and servant of all." (Mark 9:33–35)

I wonder if John, the "runt" of the disciples, always got an extra dose of grief and putdowns from the older boys in the group. Remember, the disciples were young men, some still in their teens. The Mishnah, a collection of Jewish oral laws, describes the flow of education for first-century Jewish boys: "At five years old [one is fit] for the Scripture, at ten years the Mishnah (oral Torah, interpretations), at thirteen for the fulfilling of the commandments, at fifteen the Talmud (making Rabbinic interpretations), at eighteen the bride-chamber, at twenty pursuing a vocation, at thirty for authority (able to teach others)."[3] After entering school between the ages of five and seven, a boy continued his formal education through the age of twelve or thirteen. After finishing this formal education, he could go on to sit at the feet of a teacher, perhaps following the teacher for a long period of time.[4] From what we know about John, he may have been at the younger end of the age spectrum.

I am both a younger brother and an older brother. My older brother ditched me for his friends and dished out some older-brother scorn plenty of times. I returned the favor to my younger brother. None of it was gentle, and at the time, it wasn't in good fun. In fact, we got pretty vicious with each other. I even drew blood on a few occasions. It's not an unreasonable stretch to think that when the disciples started to argue about who was the greatest, young John was probably excluded from the running right away. The louder and stronger guys probably took the lead as they shouted down John's smaller voice and pushed his weak frame out of contention. Then Mark 9:36–37 tells us that Jesus took action in the middle of the fracas:

> And [Jesus] took a child and put him in the midst of them, and taking him in His arms, He said to them, "Whoever receives one such child in My name receives Me, and whoever receives Me, receives not Me but Him who sent Me."

Remember what's happening here. Jesus called the Twelve to Himself as they gathered in a house in Capernaum. It was Jesus and the disciples gathered together for an attitude adjustment discussion. Then Jesus took a child and stood him in the middle of the group. I wonder if the "child" was John. Picked-on, outcast, bullied, weak, young John. The Greek word for "child" in these verses is *paidion*. In classical Greek, this word usually refers to a child under the age of seven. But in New Testament Greek, there is a bit more latitude. In Luke 1:76, the word refers to the baby John the Baptist. In Luke 2:17, *paidion* refers to baby Jesus. But in Matthew

17, we hear about the boy healed after Jesus was transfigured. He is referred to as a *pais*, a Greek word for a child around twelve years of age. The same account in Mark 9 refers to the boy as a *paidion*. Clearly, the word has more age flexibility in the New Testament. John may have been the *paidion* Jesus placed into the middle of the argumentative disciples. John may have been the boy Jesus took in His arms, showing His disciples what it really meant to be the greatest and defending the lowest and least of the disciples.

I wonder if that is why the apostle John referred to himself as "the disciple Jesus loved" (see John 13:23; 19:26; 20:2; 21:7). I wonder if young John experienced the grace of Jesus in a powerful way as the Savior stood up for him and stayed close to him.

I can't be sure about it, but it would be consistent with Jesus' care for the poor and disenfranchised, the weak and the outcast, the sinner and "the least of these." It may explain why the apostle John's message of love saturates his later epistles to believers. John experienced the fullness of Jesus' love—even to the point of witnessing Jesus' death and resurrection. The bold mission of showing self-sacrificial love, Christlike love, was planted deeply into his heart and soul.

BEFRIENDING THE WORLD

It is a mission each of us needs to realize more fully as we live our lives. Too often, our "Christian mission" is seen in large part as going to the far corners of the earth to evangelize civilizations that have not been reached with the Gospel. Or it is seen as serving in a soup kitchen or homeless shelter. Or it may be seen as going door to door with a readiness to share the Good News about Jesus. These are all very worthy outreach activities. But sometimes, as we visualize the mission calling God has for our lives, we forget the simple but very challenging calling to love people as Jesus first loved us.

The apostle Paul applied this to marriage when he said, "Husbands, love your wives, as Christ loved the church and gave Himself up for her" (Ephesians 5:25). The apostle Paul called husbands to total self-sacrifice—the true definition of love. What if we truly heeded the words of Jesus when He summed up the greatest commandments that all of the Scriptures rest upon?

> You shall love the Lord your God with all your heart and with all your soul and with all your mind. This is the great and first commandment. And a second is like it: You shall love your neighbor as yourself. On these two commandments depend all the Law and the Prophets. (Matthew 22:37–40)

What if unfrightened, no-strings-attached, generous, and truly kind love was the way you treated your spouse, your children, your parents, your co-workers, your neighbors, people in traffic, people who annoy you and rub you the wrong way, and people who have a completely different point of view? What would it look like? What would it mean for your words and actions?

This is a bold mission. It is a mission that follows in the steps of Jesus (1 Peter 2:21). It is one that opens the door for the communication of the Gospel. It is a mission that causes your life to be different, your choices to be adjusted, and your priorities to be realigned. What might bold love lead you to do?

Throughout history, the Church has been in danger of leaving "the least of these" behind. The people of Israel cheated the poor and downtrodden. The Church during Jesus' day rejected Him, scorned His followers, and put Him to death. Even now, the Church can easily become a place where insiders gather, where the elite meet, and where the successful come together. "Outsiders" who are not familiar with the customs, the language, or the protocols can be looked down upon and pushed away. But church people have no reason to feel superior or boast. We who were once dead in sins and transgressions but have been made alive with Christ by His grace have nothing to boast about. We corpses made alive again can take no credit or claim any superiority. We whose filthy rags of sin have been turned into righteousness by God's grace cannot look down our noses at anybody. In fact, church people are a minority these days. Where I live, only 20 percent of the population thinks it is important to attend a weekend worship service. That means eight out of ten people walking around Walmart are not thinking about church. These days, people have drifted far from God. They do not know the Bible. So many are immersed in sexual aberration, total belief in evolutionary theory, and a completely secular worldview. What does it mean to show Christ's love to this kind of culture, to a population that is living under the world's turbulent and life-draining spell? Should Christians demand that each person get his or her act together before connecting with the community of believers? Should "the least of these" be written off, or is there a way to let Jesus' love reach, transform, and bring life?

Jesus was called a "friend of sinners" (see Matthew 11:19; Luke 7:34). Perhaps that is where we are called to start: learning what it means to be a friend of sinners and of the world. Jesus told a parable about a dishonest manager who, knowing he was about to be fired, decreased the bills of his master's debtors. The master praised the dishonest manager for his strategy. He made many friends who owed him big favors. Jesus closed out the story by saying:

> The sons of this world are more shrewd in dealing
> with their own generation than the sons of light. And
> I tell you, make friends for yourselves by means of un-
> righteous wealth, so that when it fails they may receive
> you into the eternal dwellings. (Luke 16:8–9)

Jesus admitted that people of the world are really good at making friends with the culture, even in adverse circumstances. He ex-
horted believers to get good at reaching the current generation, to
make friends with the world so the relationship can become one
that leads to eternal life. The Friend of Sinners invites us to walk in
His footsteps, taking the risk of drawing close to the "sinners" of
our day, in order to see what the living Word might do in their lives
and for their eternity.

How can the Church—and how can you—befriend "sinners" for
Christ's sake? How can we do a really good job with people trapped
in sexual sin? How might we excel at befriending people who have
no idea about the Bible or the Church? What would it look like to
take the bold risk of truly loving the outcast, the unwanted, and the
least of these? What would it mean to sacrifice our comfort levels so
we could reach those outside the kingdom of God?

I know one thing: believers aren't meant to be bullies; they are
friends of the Savior, called to befriend the lost. Jesus said, "Greater
love has no one than this, that someone lay down his life for his
friends. You are My friends if you do what I command you. No
longer do I call you servants, for the servant does not know what
his master is doing; but I have called you friends, for all that I have
heard from My Father I have made known to you" (John 15:13–15).

The One who befriended us with His life, death, and resurrection calls us to befriend others with His grace and truth.

Sharing the Craved Life

What does that mean for you? It means people are waiting for you to bring something the world could never bring. The apostle Paul described how captivating the gift of life and salvation in Jesus really is and how this gift gives us a new and exciting calling as Christ's ambassadors:

> For the love of Christ controls us, because we have concluded this: that one has died for all, therefore all have died; and He died for all, that those who live might no longer live for themselves but for Him who for their sake died and was raised. From now on, therefore, we regard no one according to the flesh. Even though we once regarded Christ according to the flesh, we regard Him thus no longer. Therefore, if anyone is in Christ, he is a new creation. The old has passed away; behold, the new has come. All this is from God, who through Christ reconciled us to Himself and gave us the ministry of reconciliation; that is, in Christ God was reconciling the world to Himself, not counting their trespasses against them, and entrusting to us the message of reconciliation. Therefore, we are ambassadors for Christ, God making His appeal through us. (2 Corinthians 5:14–20)

People receive enough bad news: the reporter's coverage of another act of violence, the doctor's diagnosis of cancer, the surgeon's report that a loved one didn't make it. People are overwhelmed with bills and busyness. They are heavy laden with depression and purposelessness. They are caught in addictions and conflict. But they crave something better. What if followers of Jesus displayed kindness and love that made heads turn to the Savior? What if Christians countered conflict with compassion and grim news with glad tidings? What if the Church cared so deeply about the lost that it did everything possible—boldly stepping into a messy and risky world—to share the reason for the hope we have in the mysterious and gracious God who made His dwelling with us in the person of Jesus Christ? What if our words and deeds convinced the world that God has come close with life-changing grace?

This is what He has done. For people famished, He has come near with the life we crave.

Notes

1. news.msn.com/science-technology/mars-one-seeks-a-few-daring-souls-for-one-way-ticket-to-red-planet?ocid=msnnws; news.msn.com/science-technology/mission-shortlists-over-1000-candidates-for-life-on-mars

2. Steve Friedman, "Bret Unbroken," *Runner's World* (Emmaus, PA: Rodale, June 2013), 80–90, 127–28.

3. followtherabbi.com/guide/detail/rabbi-and-talmidim

4. Shmuel Safrai, *The Jewish People in the First Century* (Amsterdam: Van Gorcum, 1974), vol. 2, 953.

5. Paul McCain, ed., *Concordia: The Lutheran Confessions*, second edition (St. Louis: Concordia Publishing House, 2006), 440.

STUDY GUIDE FOR CHAPTER EIGHT

YOUR BOLD MISSION

1. Read Matthew 28:16–20. Discuss all the aspects of what you see Jesus commanding in these verses.

In his Large Catechism, Martin Luther emphasized the urgency of making disciples: "We should do this in order that they also may bring up their children successfully, so that God's Word and the Christian Church may be preserved."[5]

2. What opportunities do you have to do this with people in your life?

3. Read Psalm 78:1–7. In what ways might you and your church help reach the community around you with the glorious and praiseworthy deeds of the Lord?

4. Read 1 Peter 3:15. What hope do you have? How can you be ready to share it?

5. If your church has a mission statement, review it and discuss how it meshes with the bold mission Jesus gives us and what it means for you as a servant of God.

6. Read Matthew 5:13–16. Discuss ways you can befriend people God has placed in your life so "that they may see your good works and give glory to your Father who is in heaven" (v. 16).

7. How can the Church better befriend the community and the culture?

8. People always recommend good places and people to others: good restaurants, capable plumbers, their favorite hair stylists, and much more. "Word of mouth" is the best advertising for people in business. Talk about what your recommendation for Jesus would be like, the reasons you would give for recommending Him highly, and how a "word of mouth" movement might take hold in your community.

9. People crave a life that connects with much more than merely what the world offers. They crave a life with meaning, fullness, purpose, and love. Now that you've read this book, how would you say that a life of faith in Jesus Christ is that kind of life—the life people really need and, by God's grace, the life people crave?

How to Use This Book for Personal Growth

If you are just starting out in your walk of faith in Jesus Christ, or if you want to be refreshed in the essentials of your faith, this book can help you on your journey.

1. As you read chapter 1, pay close attention to the passionate love of God for you. He has a deep desire to connect with you, to be your Friend, and to serve as your Savior from sin. This is a completely unique characteristic of the Christian faith revealed by God in the Bible. Instead of having to achieve peace or measure up to a divine standard on your own, God sent His Son to rescue and help you.

2. Chapter 2 unfolds the character of God: Father, Son, and Holy Spirit. He reaches into your life with eternal hope and salvation.

3. Chapter 3 shows you how God not only enables you to live forever in His grace, but also how He gives you a new life now. He shapes you into a person who displays His character and who lives well.

4. Chapter 4 opens the door to the gift of prayer. God gives this precious gift of communication with Him and teaches you how to pray.

5. Chapter 5 shares the restoring gift of casting your cares on God as you confess your sins. You no longer have to shoulder your burdens and failures.

6. Chapter 6 explores the gift of Baptism and shows you how this reach of God into your life gives you the blessing of new life in Jesus.

7. Chapter 7 looks at the miraculous gift of the Lord's Supper and how God connects with you and sustains you through this sacred meal.

8. Chapter 8 calls you to share the beautiful, mysterious, and life-giving gifts of God with people in your life. Your prayers, actions, and conversations have the eternal purpose of making God's difference for others.

As you read this book, you'll see that God provides the life you crave. By His grace—His undeserved and generous love—God blesses you with what you really need. Use the study questions at the end of each chapter individually or in a group to explore the precious blessings God provides as you read, pray, and study.

How to Use This Book
for a Church New-Member Class

If you are leading a new-member class or a faith foundations class, this book can help you explore the central teachings of the Christian faith and discover the fullness of God's gifts in Jesus Christ. Each participant can read *The Life You Crave* and participate in discussion and teaching around each chapter's content. The class can be organized into eight sessions over a period of weeks or in a several-hour retreat format.

1. Chapter 1 answers the question "Why Jesus?" He is revealed as the only Savior from sin and death. World religions and ideologies offer self-help, rules, and theories, but they do not offer a Savior. The Christian faith is totally unique as God reveals His amazing grace and eternal love for us in Jesus Christ. A discussion about the Bible as God's revealed Word and the rhythm of Law and Gospel can be a helpful supplement to this chapter.

2. Chapter 2 looks at who God is as Father, Son, and Holy Spirit. Supplemental discussion about how and why God revealed Himself as the Trinity will help build on this chapter. A discussion of the Apostles' Creed is in the study guide following the chapter.

3. Chapter 3 outlines the new life God gives. The Ten Commandments help explain the blessing of life in Jesus Christ and what it means to be a Christian. Social issues that dovetail with the Ten Commandments can be discussed in this section.

4. Chapter 4 utilizes the Lord's Prayer to discuss the gift of prayer and how a believer in Jesus can be in touch with God. The emphases of engaging in an active prayer life and how to pray are covered in this chapter. Application and connections to your church's prayer ministry can be a helpful addition to this study session.

5. Chapter 5 discusses a believer's life of confessing sins and receiving forgiveness. This powerful gift allows a follower of Jesus to live in freedom, casting every care upon the Lord. Learning to honestly confess sin and to trust in Christ's forgiveness not only liberates the soul, but also prepares a person for reception of the Lord's Supper.

6. Chapter 6 examines how God reaches into our lives through Baptism. The biblical witness for Baptism shows that it is God's gift and action for the people He loves dearly. Discussions about the history of Baptism, the ancient practice of infant Baptism, and your local congregation's baptismal practice can supplement this chapter.

7. Chapter 7 unfolds the blessing of the Lord's Supper. Placed into the whole biblical framework, this Holy Meal is seen as part of the consistent action of God for His people throughout history. The understanding of and preparation for Holy Communion are covered in this chapter. Your local practice can supplement your study.

8. Chapter 8 covers the mission God gives to His people. It emphasizes the purpose of the believer in the world. Using your congregation's mission statement and discussing the opportunities people have to serve their families, their friends, people in the community, and people in the congregation can help develop this discussion.

This book uses the biblical Book of Daniel as a foundational text. This and the many scriptural accounts and references contained in the book will help class members appreciate the Bible's practical and life-giving message. You can use the study questions at the end of each chapter to form a discussion-based study time. These questions can be supplemented with the additional information you bring to each chapter.

About the Author

Michael Newman has served as a pastor and Bible teacher for more than twenty-five years. He enjoys communicating the gift of hope in Jesus Christ through writing, preaching, teaching, and creative mission outreach. In his personal moments, you'll find him hanging out with his family, reading a good book,  and running the Texas roads. He currently serves as a mission strategist for the Texas District of The Lutheran Church—Missouri Synod, working to share God's grace with people who need the Good News. Michael has been married to Cindy since 1983. They have been blessed with two wonderful daughters and a delightful granddaughter.

For more information, or to contact the author, go to www.mnewman.org.